Mario Reading was brought up in England and the South of France, and speaks four languages. He studied Comparative Literature under Malcolm Bradbury and Angus Wilson at the University of East Anglia, where he specialised in French and German literature and translation. During a passionately misspent youth he sold rare books, taught riding in Africa, studied dressage in Vienna, played professional polo in India, Spain and Dubai, helped run his Mexican wife's coffee plantation, and survived a terminal diagnosis for cancer. He is an award-winning author of two novels, *The Music-Makers* and *The Honourable Soldier*, and of the highly personal *Dictionary Of Cinema*.

NOSTRADAMUS

THE COMPLETE
PROPHECIES FOR THE
FUTURE

BY

MARIO READING

WATKINS PUBLISHING
LONDON

First published in the UK 2006 by
Watkins Publishing, Sixth Floor, Castle House,
75-76 Wells Street, London W1T 3QH
Distributed in the United States and Canada by
Sterling Publishing Co., Inc.
387 Park Avenue South, New York, NY 10016-8810

Reprinted 2007, 2008

5 7 9 10 8 6

Designed and typeset by Jerry Goldie

Printed and bound in China

Library of Congress Cataloging-in-Publication data available

ISBN-10: 1-84293-180-6
ISBN-13: 9-781842-931806

www.watkinspublishing.co.uk

CONTENTS

Power will be given

to overcautious fools...

NOSTRADAMUS

QUATRAIN NUMBER

2 / 9 5

ACKNOWLEDGMENTS

A number of people have helped in the preparation of this book, and I should like to take this opportunity to thank them. My editor, Michael Mann, for his patience and wise counsel, which included the inspired suggestion of the summaries; my agent, Anthea Morton-Saner, for hanging in with me through thick and thin (mostly thin); Dr Gerald Phillipson, for his suggestions on the Kabbalah; Shelagh Boyd, for her enlightened copy-editing; Penny Stopa, for her tactful help with the production details; Ned Halley (another Nostradamus nut) for his cheerful barracking; and my wife, Claudia, for her loving support and encouragement.

For my sister, Angela

INTRODUCTION

Founded in 1865 to combat currency counterfeiting and forgery, the United States Secret Service has safeguarded every US president since 1901, the year in which William McKinley became the third president to be assassinated within a period of thirty-six years. This most practised of security services has lost only one further president in the century following its inception – I am speaking of John F Kennedy, whose assassination on the 22nd November 1963 changed the world, and ushered in a whole new era of political paranoia.

There have been a number of close calls since then, with the attempt on President Truman (which resulted in the death of Officer Leslie Coffelt) and the wounding of Ronald Reagan being only the most prominent, but, on the whole, the Secret Service has been remarkably effective in protecting US Heads of State and their families from harm – with the notable but understandable exception of President Kennedy's brother, Robert, who was shot dead in Los Angeles, in 1968.

It will be an uncomfortable experience, therefore, but hardly more than that, for President George W Bush to open this book and discover that a diviner in sixteenth-century France has foreseen the attempted assassination of a major world leader as occurring sometime during his tenure. If Mr Bush is a wise man (and we must assume that he is), he will read the quatrain 10/26 – 2006–2008 very carefully indeed, and then take urgent steps to make sure the prophecy doesn't come true in relation to him.

What is new about the World Leader/Michel de Nostredame scenario, is that vulnerable world leaders with highly placed brothers will discover, on reading quatrain number 10/26, not only that an assassination attempt may be made on their lives, but also what will happen *after* the assassination – if, of course, it is successful. This information they will no doubt find hard to swallow. But we are not asking them to take it simply on trust. Just look at the track record. Nostradamus correctly predicted the death, during a friendly joust, of King Henry II of France, right down to the splintered lance of Henry's opponent entering the King's helmet through the visor and piercing his eye. Nostradamus warned Henry's Queen, Catherine de Medici, in person, of the danger, but she was unable to dissuade her husband from agreeing to a rematch (following a hung decision after their first bout) with the reluctant Montgomery, Captain of the Scottish Guard. The King died an agonising death, ten days later, on the 10th July 1559. The crestfallen Montgomery, pardoned by the King, succumbed to the widowed Queen's disfavour a full fifteen years after her husband's death – and that, too, was predicted by Nostradamus, in quatrain 3/30, right down to the six armed men who kidnapped him, naked, from his bedroom, and hurried him to the Conciergerie prison, where he died.

Benito Mussolini, too, would have been well-advised to lend an ear to quatrain 2/24, in which not only is his death predicted, but also the manner of it described – being 'hung inside a cage of iron', which turned out to be the charred frame of a fire-bombed petrol station at Guilino di Mezzegra, near Lake Como, in Italy. Napoleon, the Duc de Berry, Charles I, Adolf Hitler, Mary, Queen of Scots, and even John F Kennedy could all have benefited from advance warning of their death, but, as Augustine Birrell so elegantly puts it, in his *Obiter Dicta*; 'History is a pageant and not a philosophy.' Even if we have knowledge of the future, it is not necessarily either desirable, or even possible to act on that information.

Now back to the *Complete Prophecies For The Future*. I have begun the commentaries marginally in the past, with the Twin Towers Disaster of the 11th September 2001, not only because it coincided almost exactly with the turn of our century, but also because Nostradamus's predictions about the event are so detailed, and so astonishing, that they will give even further credence to his prognostications for both our future, and that of our planet. Interpreting Nostradamus is very much like working on a detective story. Following his filigrees of meaning through to a final, if tentative, conclusion, is an immensely satisfying work of deduction. I have therefore taken as my starting point the premise that the most esoteric of Nostradamus's quatrains – in other words those without any obvious reference to the times in which he lived, or to the four and a half centuries immediately succeeding his death – must, by default, refer to the future. I have therefore retranslated these, and approached them entirely afresh, without referring back to past commentaries.

Old French spellings are eccentric, to say the least, and both proper names and nouns can be spelled in a variety of ways. Meanings themselves were considered far more fluid then than they would be now, and an absolutely literal interpretation of any text would have been scoffed at by educated sixteenth-century readers. What is entirely new about my approach concerns the interrelation between quatrains – one feeds from the other, as it were. By adhering to Nostradamus's own index dates when dealing with prophecies relating to the future, connections were found across *The Centuries* which threw an extraordinary collective light onto the meanings of individual, often opaque, prophecies.

Commentators in the past have approached all the quatrains individually, as separate predictions, but Nostradamus was an alchemist and a scryer, and he believed in mixing things, and from that admixture, truth would come. Alchemists believed that everything on earth was fused and inter-relatable and that one only had to discover the secret of this to reach hidden codes and morphological secrets. Many of the quatrains, although nominally stemming from different Nostradamian *Centuries*, are, in fact, closely interconnected and interrelated, and can only be correctly construed when this is borne in mind. This fact, this interrelation, only comes to light when one is in the actual process of interpreting them – one quatrain feeds off the other, and a true interpretation can only be reached when this is taken into account. Previous commentators have simply not listened enough to Nostradamus's index dating. There is even an argument, to which I give some credence, that Nostradamus may have intended the quatrains as a sort of rolling commentary on history – that he meant them to be used over and over again, in other words, and that they were only fully interpretable after the event.

Nostradamus organized his quatrains into *Centuries* of one hundred quatrains apiece (save for the seventh in the series of ten, which stops at number forty-two). It is probable that he originally intended the quatrain numbers to correspond directly to years in the calendar, but then chickened out for fear of the Inquisition. However the skeleton of his original structure still remains. Very often quatrains that may seem rather insipid if taken alone, gain in interest and clarity when taken in the context of other quatrains, appearing in different *Centuries*, but with similar index years. This is particularly true of quatrains that foretell (in Nostradamian terms, of course) the distant future. By the use of these parallels, a picture can be summoned up of a time far in the future, and of the events which invest it.

Many of the index dates link together categorically, in terms of meaning, with similar index dates in different *Centuries*, for even though many years may separate the time of writing, they still apply to the very same events. A good example would be the Global War scenario in quatrains 10/69, 5/70, 9/70, 2/70, 8/70, and 3/71, which predict events in the years 2069–2071. Another would be the French Crisis sequence of 10/98, 6/99, 1/100, 2/100, and 10/1, which cover the years 2098–2101. Or how about the Crisis In The Roman

Catholic Church series, in quatrains 2/56, 5/56, 4/56, 10/57 and 2/57, with a year span of 2056–2057? Or the End Of Monarchy In Britain cycle, of 10/40, 4/40 and 5/40, year span 2040? Look at the index dates – they are absolutely specific. As are the connections between the quatrains. And no one has noticed this before!

Far too little account has been taken, in the past, of classical references and mythologies in Nostradamus's writings. These would have formed the fundamental basis of Nostradamus's thinking processes – even the concept of the Oracle, which Nostradamus personified, was taken from that of Delphi. Nostradamus would, like any educated man in sixteenth-century France, have had a vast body of classical learning at his fingertips, and would have considered its use, and his readers' understanding of classical myth, as a *sine qua non*. A similar wellhead of knowledge needs to be used when interpreting the quatrains today, and negates any half-baked ideas that Nostradamus wrote in a secret, or Green Language, accessible only to privileged initiates, or to those versed in the secret lore of the Akashic Chronicle. He was, quite simply, extremely well read and well educated.

The French are traditionally fond of word play, and in Nostradamus's time no one would have dreamt of assuming that a word meant simply what it was purported to mean within the context of a single sentence – the larger context, too, would need to be taken into account. I'll give you an example. An apparently straightforward Old French phrase such as '*En Normandie l'on vendange avec la gaule*', which, taken literally would appear to mean, 'In Normandy they harvest with a pole', can also mean, 'In Normandy, they even harvest beside Frenchmen', or, alternatively, 'The Poles are the vintagers in Normandy'. Irritating for translators, yes, but also enormously rich in potential seams of gold and hidden meanings.

The key to Nostradamus, in my opinion, is in the actual process of translation – the act of translating opens the commentator's mind to what Nostradamus, through the centuries (both literally and metaphorically) is trying to tell him. The most important thing for a translator is never to translate line by line. The whole quatrain must always be considered, and one is often forced to return to the beginning when the final meaning becomes clear. Wishful thinking is the translator's greatest danger – the temptation to plump on one possible answer because it appears obvious. Because we commentators are not, by default, Nostradamus himself, we are condemned to approach him retrospectively. This, needless to say, sets us up for accusations of closing the stable door after the horse has bolted. By addressing only the future, I am secretly rather hoping to avoid that criticism, but I acknowledge that any commentary on Nostradamus that invokes such a future is invested by the commentator's own, inevitably limited, knowledge of the present, and the limits of the commentator's own innate imaginative capacities.

The only answer to this dilemma is for the commentator to approach the quatrains with an open mind, and the capacity to be surprised in a serendipitous manner. I trust that, when you read the commentaries which follow, you will feel that I have done this.

BIOGRAPHICAL NOTE

Nostradamus was both a Catholic and a Jew. If that sounds like a paradox, it wasn't perceived as such in a sixteenth-century France dedicated to both God, in the form of the Inquisition, and mammon, in the form of the pillaging of others' property for reasons of ecclesiastical expediency.

For thirty years, under the reign of Good King René, the Jews of Provence had been accorded the free practice of their religion, but all that ended with René's death in 1480, a date which unfortunately coincided with the inception of the Spanish Inquisition. By the time of Nostradamus's birth, in 1503, most prominent Jews had prudently converted to a pragmatic form of Catholicism, thanks to the edicts of, respectively, Charles VIII in 1488, and Louis XII in 1501. This didn't prevent the French Crown from occasionally plundering their possessions, but it did offer them a measure of protection in a country suddenly rife with religious intolerance and paranoia. So the infant Michel de Nostredame found himself both uncircumcised (the penalty for which, under Levitical Law, is ostracism from the congregation of Israel), and baptised according to the Christian Rite, while retaining, in the form of his two grandfathers, an intimate access to the Jewish chain of tradition known as the *Schalscheleth Hakabbālah*, which was to stand him in very good stead in his later incarnation as a diviner and scryer.

As a result of this upbringing, Nostradamus almost certainly dabbled in magic, and very certainly in mysticism and the Kabbalah, which encapsulated the Jewish search for new wisdom in a creative synthesis between the mythologies of ancient Egypt, ancient Greece, Assyrian astrology, Babylonian magic, Arabian divination and Platonic philosophy. The secretive and mystical nature of the Kabbalah provided a much-needed escape from the grim realities of Jewish life in an Inquisitorial Europe, and a much-needed panacea in the face of the forcible conversions that followed René's death. By pure chance, Nostradamus's native town of St Rémy was the perfect place to study the Kabbalah, as Provence was generally acknowledged as home to the earliest Kabbalistic community in France. Paradoxically, perhaps, Nostradamus, as well as being a Kabbalist, an alchemist, and a Talmudist, was also a fervent adherent to Catholic doctrine throughout his life, and would certainly not have been accepted at Avignon University (not then a part of France) had he not been sincere in these assertions, and in his excoriations of the near ubiquitous Lutheran heresy. He later enrolled, again without problem, at the venerable University of Montpellier (founded in 1220) in order to study medicine – a wise move, as Montpellier possessed, without doubt, the greatest school of medicine of those times.

Following on from his matriculation from Montpellier – which was conducted in the medieval manner of a formal, invigilated dispute between the student and the teaching staff, rather than by written examination – Nostradamus was plunged straight into the treatment of an outbreak of the plague. Encumbered by the usual paraphernalia worn by medical practitioners during such crises (leather jerkin, glasses, sponge mask, and a coat stained with many different coloured powders), Nostradamus struck out into entirely new territory with his invention of a purifying powder, which, we are led to believe, inspired an entirely untypical confidence in his patients. As a direct consequence of this experience, Nostradamus became something of an authority on the plague, a talent that was sorely tested when plague struck, once again, during his tenure as a doctor at Agen, killing his young wife and their two children. As a result, Nostradamus not only suffered from the usual criticism of 'Physician, heal thyself', but was also sued by the distraught family of his wife for the return of her dowry.

Traumatised by his loss, Nostradamus took to the road, and travelled through many parts of France, Italy and Sicily, before finally settling in Salon de Provence. There, at the age of forty-four, he met a widow, Anne Ponsarde Gemelle, whom he married on the 11th November 1547. They moved into a house on the Rue Ferreiraux (now known as Rue Nostradamus), and Nostradamus, in considerable demand by this time, not least for his sovereign remedies, continued his travels. It was during this period that, thanks to his meetings with apothecaries, physicians and magicians, he first began to suspect that he had the gift of prophecy and second sight. He was not the only one, of course. Under the reign of the thirteen Valois Kings, it was estimated that there were upwards of 30,000 astrologers, sorcerers, alchemists and prophets practising in Paris alone, and it is to Nostradamus's credit, and to that of his art, that he rose, inexorably, to the top of a very crowded tree.

Three years after the publication of his *Traité Des Fardemens* in 1552 (an *à la mode* treatise on unguents, jams and preserves of all kinds), Nostradamus followed up – rather tentatively, it must be said – with the first edition of his famous *Centuries* (1555), fearing, according to his pupil, Jean Aymes de Chavigny, both castigation and mockery. The three hundred and fifty-three quatrains, to just about everybody's surprise, including that of Nostradamus, were a sensation. Summoned to Paris by Henri II's Queen, Catherine de Medici, barely a year after publication, Nostradamus returned to Salon a rich man, having discovered, the hard way, that private practice (the casting of personal horoscopes and the alleviation of courtiers' ailments) was considerably more remunerative, and a good deal less precarious, than celebrity stargazing.

Nostradamus continued to advise Catherine, though, not least because she protected him, in some measure, from falling foul of the religious authorities for blasphemy, while her regal favour afforded him a much-appreciated kudos and the promise of a steady income. The summit of his celebrity career came during a royal visit to Salon itself, in 1564, by the boy king, Charles IX (who would later, at his dominant mother's instigation, approve the St Bartholomew's Day Massacre). Catherine invited Nostradamus and his family to a private visit at the royal apartments, and then to a further consultation, where she asked him to cast the horoscope of her youngest son, the Duke of Anjou. Nostradamus was more interested in the young Henri de Navarre, however, and even investigated the ten-year-old child while he was sleeping, predicting that he would eventually inherit all of France.

Nostradamus was well paid for his troubles, which must have provided considerable comfort during his two declining years, for, assailed by gout, arthritis and a heart condition that even his own sovereign remedies failed to alleviate, he finally succumbed on the 2nd July 1566, in exactly the fashion he had predicted for himself.

THE
PROPHECIES

TWIN TOWERS DISASTER I

SEPTEMBER 2001

1/87

Ennosigée, feu du centre de terre,

Fera trembler au tour de Cité Neufve;

Deux grands rochers long temps feront la guerre,

Puis Arethusa rougira nouveau Fleuve.

✸

Earthshaking, a fire from the centre of the earth

Will shake the towers of the New City

As a result, two great rocks will fight a long war

Until Arethusan springs bloody the river afresh.

An uncanny foretelling of the Twin Towers disaster, even down to a paralleling of the two rock-like towers with a war between the 'two great rocks' of Christianity and Islam. The towers are brought down by fire drawn from the earth's core, an extraordinary leap of the imagination for Nostradamus when one bears in mind that the explosive catalyst used in the attacks was oil-based aviation fuel. Another extraordinary coincidence links the myth of Arethusa, with her legendary springs at Ellis, to that of Ellis Island, the immigration gateway to New York – a buried clue left by Nostradamus which pinpoints exactly to which New City he is referring in his text.

A further clue to the location of the disaster is contained in the first line's use of the word *du*, which can mean either 'of' or 'from'. If read as 'fire *of* the centre of the earth', then the World Trade Centre tellingly springs to mind. Nostradamus's use of the term *Cité Neufve* (the New City), immediately links 1/87 to the next quatrain in our series, 10/49 – 2001. Other similarities also grab the attention; the mention of rocks and mountains; the symbols of water and its poisoning, the first time with blood, the second with sulphur; and the Arethusan springs, at both Ellis and Syracuse (also a place in New York State).

SUMMARY

Following an attack on New York's Twin Towers, in which aviation fuel is the principle component, a long war between Christianity and Islam is triggered.

TWIN TOWERS DISASTER II

SEPTEMBER 2001

10/49

Jardin du monde au pres du cité neufve,

Dans le chemin des montaignes cavees,

Sera saisi et plongé dans la Cuve,

Beuvant par force eaux soulfre envenimees.

❂

The world's garden near the New City

In the roadway, hollow mountains,

They will be seized, and plunged into the sewers

People will be forced to drink the sulphur-poisoned waters.

PREDICTION

A chilling image of the Twin Towers, which Nostradamus describes, in the only way he is able, given the limitations of the period in which he is living, as 'hollow mountains in the roadway'. We already know, from 1/87 – 2001, that his 'New City' is New York. Here he presents a terrifying picture of the two skyscrapers being 'plunged into the sewers', descriptions that could have been taken direct from television news pictures of the disaster showing the towers crumpling inexorably earthwards. 'Sulphur-poisoned waters' can be taken both figuratively and as a metaphor for the realization, by the United States, that from this moment on, they, too, are vulnerable, and that they will be forced to drain the cup of poisoned water fate has handed them to its dregs.

SUMMARY

The destruction of the Twin Towers will traumatize the people of the United States. There will be many long-term effects of the tragedy, and it will poison relations between the US and Islam.

GUANTANAMO BAY

2002 ONWARDS

I/59

Les exilez deportez dans les isles,
Au changement d'un plus cruel monarque
Seront meurtris: et mis deux les scintiles,
Qui de parler ne seront estez parques.

❋

The exiles are deported to the islands

When the new leader proves even crueller

There are murders; two at a time they will be
questioned

Until they cannot stop speaking.

More than five hundred political detainees were transferred from Camp X-Ray to the newly built Camp Delta at Guantanamo Bay (which forms part of the Cuban archipelago, ergo 'the islands') following the defeat of the Taliban in Afghanistan in 2002. After the US/Iraq war of 2003, even more 'exiles' were transferred there. In Ba'athist terms, President Bush would be perceived as an even 'crueller' leader than Saddam Hussein, and countless murders have been committed as a direct result of US intervention in both countries. The Bush regime, embarrassed by the bad publicity over its treatment of the internees, has since struggled to establish a legally viable argument to justify its harsh interrogation techniques at Guantanamo, which, as one US official dryly commented, is the 'legal equivalent of outer space'. It is reasonable to suppose that prisoners, on the receiving end of such techniques, would very often talk 'until they cannot stop speaking'.

SUMMARY

Survivors of the war in Afghanistan are deported to Guantanamo Bay. One prisoner's testimony is used against the other. The prisoners, under intolerable pressure, are eventually forced to talk.

US/IRAQ WAR I

MARCH/APRIL 2003

7/7

Sur le combat des grans cheveux, legiers

On criera le grand croissant confond

De nuict tuer monts, habits de bergiers

Abismes rouges dans le fossé profond.

❋

As a result of the war started by the mighty light-haired ones

People will cry out that the great crescent of Islam is confounded

At night, on the mountains, those dressed as shepherds will die

Gulleys of blood will run through the deep ditches.

An accurate foretelling of the war which occurred between the United States with its ally the United Kingdom (the mighty light-haired ones), and Iraq, during March and April 2003. Nostradamus implies that it will be wrongly assumed, following the conflict, that the might of Islam has been tamed. A terrible bloodbath will follow, with many Iraqis killed. Nostradamus's haunting image of blood running through the 'deep ditches' may suggest, as happened in Afghanistan during the war of October 2001, that a return to trench warfare will form part of the continuing conflict. If taken metaphorically, of course, the symbol of a 'ditch' accurately portrays the vast gulf remaining between both sides of the conflict, a gulf that will rapidly fill up with the dead and dying.

SUMMARY

The war against Islam will not be easily won by the Western powers. Many will die before an accommodation is reached. There will be times when the fighting reaches unprecedented levels of brutality.

US/IRAQ WAR II

MARCH/APRIL 2003

6/34

Du feu volant la machination

Viendra troubler au grand chef assiegez

Dedans sera telle sedition

Qu'en desespoir seront les profligez.

✳

The contrivance of flying fire

Will come to trouble the besieged leader

Inside, there will be so much sedition

That the corrupt ones will despair.

This has a pretty clear connection with 6/97 – 2003 [US/Iraq War III], with its use of the 'flying fire' and 'burning sky' analogies, together with the implication of a 'besieged' city, and its leader. By the end of his twenty-four-year hold on power, Saddam Hussein had become completely 'corrupt', and his autocracy knew, quite literally, no bounds. It is also perfectly possible to read line 1's 'contrivance of flying fire' as implying that Hussein would encounter problems with weapons of mass destruction, and that these would contribute to his downfall. We do know that he viciously put down all 'sedition' within the ranks of his Ba'athist party, even going so far as to have members of his own immediate family killed for disloyalty. All these factors, once taken together, make the quatrain particularly impressive.

SUMMARY

Saddam Hussein will be attacked from the sky. His own people will rise against him. He will belatedly recognize the mistakes he has made, but it will be too late to change the outcome of the attack.

US/IRAQ WAR III

MARCH/APRIL 2003

6/97

Cinq et quarante degrés ciel bruslera,

Feu approcher de la grand cité neufve,

Instant grand flamme esparse sautera,

Quand on voudra des Normans faire preuve.

✹

The sky will burn those at 45 degrees

Fire will approach the great new city

All of a sudden a thick wall of flame will leap
upwards

When they ask for proof from the Northerners.

'45 degrees' north runs pretty much plumb through the centre of Baghdad, which could indeed, back in 2003, have been construed as 'the great new city', given the enormous amount of building work undertaken, since the Gulf War of 1991, at the behest of the vainglorious Saddam Hussein. We know Nostradamus means the northern rather than the southern latitudes because of his mention of 'Normans', in line 4, which was a common euphemism at the time for those from the north.

It is certainly true that, for an unconscionably long time, Saddam Hussein, suffering, no doubt, from Dictator Denial Syndrome, chose to believe that the US and their British and Australian Allies ('the Northerners') would not attack Baghdad itself – rather as Hitler once believed that Churchill would not declare war on Germany, and Stalin once believed that Hitler would honour the Nazi/Soviet non-aggression pact. The US then used what they called 'shock and awe' tactics on the 20th March, and great walls of flame did indeed 'leap upwards' from all around Baghdad city, in a massive display of military firepower. The initial campaign was declared formally over by President Bush on the 1st May 2003, paving the way for the much longer and more prickly transition towards a peaceful democracy.

SUMMARY

Saddam Hussein, playing a dangerous game of brinkmanship, finds his bluff called. Baghdad is bombed, and his regime is ended.

US/IRAQ WAR IV

2003 ONWARDS

5/4

Le gros mastin de cité deschassé
Sera fasché de l'etrange alliance
Apres aux champs avoir le cerf chassé
Le lous et l'Ours se donront defiance.

✿

The great hound is driven from the city

Importuned by the foreign alliance

The stag is harried from the field

The wolf and the bear will defy each other.

The 'great hound' is Saddam Hussein, driven from his city, Baghdad, by the 'foreign alliance' of the United States and the United Kingdom, and finally captured, in December 2003, in the small town of Al-Dawr, living six feet underground, in a hole. The image of the hole leads us to an amusing clue hidden inside this bestiary of a quatrain, for the 'stag' is the traditional symbol for Christ, and stems from its habit (according to Pliny's *Natural History*) of drawing serpents, by its breath, from their burrows, and then trampling them to death.

We also know that the ancient Christian community in Iraq (represented by the 'stag') is being driven out of the country to eventual extinction, further deepening the animal revocations. The 'bear', needless to say, is Russia, and the 'wolf' (an animal traditionally dedicated to Odin, the giver of victory) is the United States. These two powers are facing off over Iraq and its oil reserves, with the US accusing Russia of acting illegally in annexing the privatised oil company, Yukos, and Russia riposting with accusations that the US was only interested in liberating Iraq on account of its own long-term energy needs. So, alongside the hound, the stag, the wolf, the bear, and the snake, we can now add a bevy of fossils to further fuel Nostradamus's animal menagerie.

SUMMARY

Saddam Hussein is discovered hiding in a hole, like an animal. His fall will not be the end of the story, however. It will trigger further disasters, including the destruction of what remains of the ancient Christian community in Iraq.

BURMA'S MILITARY JUNTA

2003 ONWARDS

4/41

Gymnique sexe captive par hostage

Viendra de nuit custodes decevoir

Le chef du camp deceu par son langage

Lairra à la gente, sera piteux à voir.

✻

A captive of the female sex

Will come by night; her guards will be deceived

The leader, angered by her tongue

Hands her to the people; it will be pitiful to see.

The most famous female political prisoner of the twenty-first century, and winner of the Nobel Peace Prize in 1991, is Burma's Aung San Sun Kyi. Elected leader of Burma (Myanmar) by a landslide victory in 1990, she has suffered house arrest in Rangoon (Yangon) on three separate occasions – for six years, from 1989 to 1995; for a further twenty months, until May 2002; and then again, for the third time, from May 2003. The military junta that has ruled Burma from 1962 are, indeed, 'angered by her tongue', and her guards have been 'deceived' into imprisoning her against the will of the people. Nostradamus foretells a time when she will be handed back to the people, triggering a tragedy. Whether this will be in the form of a civil war, or an assassination, is unclear. A third possibility does arise, however, which would see her 'handing back to the people' as the trigger for a different sort of 'pitiful' event – that of the timely end of one of the few remaining totalitarian regimes in the region through the forces of mass insurrection.

SUMMARY

The elected president of Burma, Aung San Sun Kyi, will be released from house arrest. This signals the beginning of the end of the current Burmese regime. Mass insurrection will follow, and many innocent people will die.

TSUNAMI I

26TH DECEMBER 2004

1/29

Quand le poisson, terrestre et aquatique,

Par forte vague au gravier sera mis,

Sa forme étrange suave et horrifique

Par mer aux murs bien tort enemies.

❈

When fish, both land and sea-based

Are thrown onshore by strong waves

Their strangely smooth, yet horrifying appearance

Will make of the twisted walls our enemy.

The force of the floods Nostradamus is describing will be powerful enough to drive maritime fish, never before seen in such a place, into the cities. The terrible deluge which caused their coming will mean that the ancient city 'walls', together with the 'walls' of people's houses, originally built to protect them, will now become threats. His accurate description of a tidal wave, or tsunami, as 'strangely smooth', is all the more haunting because such a concept would have been entirely outside his own experience.

The image of the smooth walls of water suddenly turning into a threat recall to mind the younger Pliny's letters to Tacitus (Epistle vi 16, 20), and his description of the tidal waves which struck Herculaneum after the eruption of Vesuvius, in August 79 AD. As well as destroying Pompeii and Stabiae, the monstrous waves also killed his uncle, the elder Pliny, whose name the former Publius Caecilius Secundus then took through adoption. A similar earthquake, magnitude 9.0 on the Richter scale, occurred off the west coast of Northern Sumatra, Indonesia, at 00.58.33 UTC, on the 26th December 2004, at the interface of the Indian and Burma plates. Maritime fish were, indeed, found on dry land after the disaster, and the 'walls' of the shifting tectonic plates did, undeniably, become our 'enemy'.

SUMMARY

A tsunami wave, triggered by a massive underwater earthquake, will ravage Indonesia and the surrounding areas.

MIDDLE EAST PEACE INITIATIVE

9TH JANUARY 2005 ONWARDS

8/59

Par deux fois hault, par deux fois mis à bas

L'orient aussi l'occident faiblira

Son adversaire apres plusieurs combats

Par mer chassé au besoin faillira.

✳

Twice raised high, and twice-clad Abbas

The East will weaken, and the West, too

After many battles its adversary

Will be driven into the sea and fail, just when needed.

Nostradamus often hid the name of key characters, who would later take their places in world history, somewhere within his quatrains. Here, in the first line, we have *à bas*, which, in Old French, would be pronounced 'abbass'. The word *mis*, too, can have a number of meanings, one of which is 'clad', or 'anointed'. Thus we are led to Mahmoud Abbas (a.k.a. Abu Mazen), who was raised high, for the second time, on the 9th January 2005, by being elected president of the Palestinian Authority (following the death of Yasser Arafat) by a record sixty-two per cent of the electorate. His initial 'raising' and 'anointing' had occurred in March 2003, when he had been elected first Prime Minister of the Palestinian Authority – but at that time Abbas resigned after only four months in office, through frustration at being perceived as Arafat's puppet. Nostradamus goes on to imply that both the Middle East 'and the West, too' will need to weaken – meaning, in this context, to move one towards the other. The 'adversary' mentioned here is, by implication, any adversary of peace, and Nostradamus sees these elements (both Islamic and Jewish), failing in their undermining of the peace process at the exact needed moment, and being, in consequence, 'driven into the sea'.

SUMMARY

Mahmoud Abbas, the new Palestinian leader, will succeed, where others before him have failed, in securing a peaceful settlement in the Middle East.

DEATH OF POPE JOHN PAUL II

2ND APRIL 2005

8 / 46

Pol mensolee mourra trois lieus du Rosne

Fuis les deux prochains tarasc destrois

Car Mars fera le plus horrible trosne

De coq et d'aigle de France, freres trois.

✸

The celibate Pole (Paul) will die in three places in Rome

The next two flee the oppressive monster

Because Mars will occupy the papal throne

For the cock and the eagle of France, three brothers.

Nostradamus was particularly fond of predicting the deaths of popes, and here is his prediction of the death of Pope John Paul II (Karol Wojtyla), or 'the celibate Pole', at exactly 19.37 hours GMT, on Saturday 2nd April 2005. The pope did, indeed, die in 'three places in Rome': his private apartments at the Vatican; in St Peter's Square, when his death was announced to the crowds; and in the crypt of St Peter's Basilica, where he is now buried. In addition, the Italian authorities immediately declared 'three' days of national mourning. The significance of the word 'three' is reiterated in line 4, with the 'three brothers'. Man is, of course, threefold, with the body, the soul, and the spirit, and his enemies, too, are threefold, consisting of the world, the flesh, and the devil. Even the Christian Graces are threefold, in Faith, Hope, and Charity, and there are three books of the Bible, consisting of the Old Testament, the New Testament, and the Apocrypha. 'Three' is the perfect number, according to Pythagoras, symbolic of a beginning, a middle, and an end, and three wise kings, Melchior, Gaspar and Balthazar, visited the infant Jesus in the stable. The Magi (the 'three brothers' in line 4) is taken, in Camoëns's *Lusiad*, to mean the same as the Indian word Brahmin, and we know that Brahma was one of the three beings created by God to assist in the creation of the world – thus proving the interconnectedness of every myth, every dogma, and every theocracy under the sun.

The 'oppressive monster', Tarascon, part lion, part crocodile, was tamed by Saint Martha, the patron saint of housewives, and she is traditionally shown with a bunch of keys at her girdle, symbolically equating with the papal keys of St Peter. The power of the keys (Matthew xvi. 19) is the supreme authority vested in the pope as the successor to St Peter, and one cannot help wondering if the next two popes who flee the 'oppressive monster' are not in fact fleeing the threat of female emancipation within the Catholic Church, as personified by St Martha? Either way, Mars, the God of War (but also of Divine Fortitude, the guardian power of Christianity) appears to occupy the papal throne for the period of these two papacies, and as both the cock and the eagle are traditionally viewed as male icons, as are the 'three brothers' of the Magi, so it seems likely that the traditional teachings of the Catholic Church will ultimately prevail.

Summary

Following the death of Pope John Paul II, the next two popes will continue along the conservative path he blazed, opposing women priests, contraception, and abortion.

NEW ORLEANS FLOODS

AUGUST/SEPTEMBER 2005

3 / 84

La grand cité sera bien desolee,

Des habitans un seul n'y demoura

Mur, sexe, temple et vierge violee,

Par fer, feu, peste, canon peuple mourra.

✷

The great city will be laid to waste

Not even one inhabitant will remain

Walls, women, churches and virgins are violated

People will die by knife, fire, plague and gunshot.

Katrina, a Category Five hurricane, began her handiwork in New Orleans (a city whose 480,000 population was two thirds black, and in which forty per cent of the children lived below the poverty line) on Monday 29th August 2005. Within two short days, eighty per cent of the urban area was ten feet under water, following the destruction of the levees built to contain Lake Pontchartrain, and rioting, looting, arson, and rape had broken out across the Crescent City, pending the imposition of martial law. And Nostradamus, here in quatrain 3/84, describes the situation exactly, right down to the evacuation of every single inhabitant of the city ('not even one inhabitant will remain'); to the knifings and rapes amongst the 60,000 refugees in the New Orleans Superbowl Stadium, including the violation of a seven-year-old girl – Nostradamus's *vierge*; to the killing of five looters on the Danziger Bridge; and, finally, to the infections arising from the pollution of the flood waters by waste toxins, dead bodies, and sewage related bacteria.

SUMMARY

Alongside the great Mississippi River flood of 1927, the 2005 New Orleans, Alabama, and Mississippi Delta flood, with its 140mph winds and twenty-five-foot storm surges covering a 90,000 square-mile area the size of the United Kingdom, was the greatest single natural disaster in US history. Go to 9/48 –2048 [US Hurricanes/Global Warming III] for the next great US environmental disaster.

DEATH OF A LEADER IN ROME

Apparoistra vers le Septentrion,
Non loin de Cancer l'estoille chevelue
Suze, Sienne, Boece, Eretrion,
Mourra de Rome grand, la nuict disparue.

❁

There will be seen, towards the North

Not far from Cancer, a beard-trailing star

Susa, Sienna, Bocche, Etruria

When the great one dies in Rome, the night will disappear.

Horace Tuttle was the first person to discover comet 41P/Tuttle-Giacobini-Kresak, way back in 1858. '41P', will begin 2006 retrograding through Orion, and then, just as Nostradamus predicts, it will swing northwards, cutting through Taurus, Gemini, Cancer, Leo and Virgo. It at first seems likely that Nostradamus was a year out in his prediction of Pope John Paul II's death. There is an alternative reading, however, and that is that the 'great one' who dies in Rome is not the pope at all, but another grandee.

The image that 'the night will disappear' is an interesting one, and causes one to wonder whether the grandee who dies might not be connected, in some way, with television? It also takes us back to Orion (*Septentrion*), and 41P. The mighty hunter Orion, noted for his manly beauty, was blinded by Oenopion, but Vulcan (the great cuckold), in an uncharacteristic fit of pity, sent Cedalion down to guide him back through his old hunting grounds. Orion's sight was eventually restored by the exposure of his eyeballs to the sun – 'the night', in other words, was made to 'disappear' – but Diana ended up by killing him, and he was made into his very own constellation, through which 41P, as we now know, will retrograde in 2006. And thereby hangs a tail.

SUMMARY

Another leader will die in Rome, but it will not necessarily be the new pope. It will be an important figure, however, and possibly someone associated with the television industry.

CRISIS IN THE
PROTESTANT CHURCH

2006

3 / 6

Dans le temple clos le foudre ʒ entrera,

Les citadins dedans leur fort grevez

Chevaux, boeufs, hommes, l'onde mur touchera,

Par faim, soif, soubs les plus faibles armez.

❋

Lightning will enter the sealed church

The people inside will be deeply aggrieved

Horses, cattle, men, the ripened wave will touch
them all

Due to hunger and thirst, even the weakest will
arm themselves.

A *temple*, in Old French, referred specifically to a Protestant church. Given this fact, it now appears that there will be a crisis, sometime in 2006, undermining the vacuum which now exists inside the Protestant convocation. This has been on the cards for some time ('ripened wave'), and will affect everything and everyone to do with the Church ('horses, cattle, men'). Sidelined, even the female members of the Church ('the weakest') will join in the argument on the side of change. Given all this, and the index date of 2006, one's thoughts inevitably turn towards the question of homosexual bishops, and the schisms beginning to appear inside the global Anglican community as a result of the appointment of the Reverend Canon Gene Robinson as the first openly gay Bishop of New Hampshire, in August 2003. Further to this, of course, is the question of female bishops, and to the schism their inception will create amongst hardliners. The telling image of the women arming themselves, in line 4, may, of course, simply refer to the assumption, by female aspirants, of the bishop's crosier, and serves us with additional remarkable testimony to Nostradamus's predictive powers.

SUMMARY

The Anglican Church will be thrown into disarray by the argument over gay clergy and female bishops. There is the distinct possibility of a permanent schism between the conservative and the liberal elements of the synod, which may result in the Church splitting into two separate congregations.

ASSASSINATION OF A WORLD LEADER

2006 ONWARDS

10/26

Le successeur vengera son beau frere,

Occupera regne souz umbre de vengeance,

Occis ostacle son sang mort vitupere,

Long temps Bretaigne tiendra avec la France.

✺

The successor will avenge his handsome brother

He will take over the realm under cover of vengeance

The obstacle slain, his dead blood seethes

Britain and France will hold together for a long time.

Given the tenor of the first two lines, in which 'vengeance' and the 'taking over of a realm' are mentioned, it seems that Nostradamus is referring to a major political assassination in this quatrain. This reading is further strengthened by the reference to Britain and France in line 4, suggesting that the events due to unfold have worldwide implications. It is tempting to assume that Nostradamus is referring to someone's brother-in-law (*beau frere*), and not to a 'handsome brother', in line 1, but the reading would be a false one. The words *beau* and *frere* are categorically unlinked, whereas they would undoubtedly be linked or hyphenated if brother-in-law were the intended meaning. A possible clue to the identity of the handsome brother lies in line 2, in the words *souz umbre* – 'under cover'. Nostradamus is referring to a place where one would seek protection when out in the wild: i.e. a under a 'bush'. Once this is grasped, the quatrain becomes a little easier to unravel, although it is still impossible to be entirely sure which world leader (with a brother already holding high office) will be the eventual assassination target.

One of many possible targets, of course, might be US President George W Bush. In such an imagined scenario, Nostradamus would appear to be positing that the president's brother – in this purely exemplary case it would be Jeb Bush, already a twice-elected Governor of Florida – would be voted in, by an outraged US electorate, in his place. Nostradamus then goes on to picture the outraged brother of the victim avenging his 'handsome' brother, but by actions that would so alienate his country's erstwhile ally, Britain, that it is driven to align itself with France (in this case standing for the whole of the European Union), an alliance which will, unlike those of the past, hold together for a long time.

Summary

An attempt is made to assassinate a powerful world leader. Should the attempt be successful, the brother of the world leader will be elected in his stead. He will take revenge for his brother's death, and this will so alienate his country's main ally, Britain, that it will be forced to turn its back on its old alliances, and align itself with the newly emerging European superstate, personified, in this instance, by France.

NORTH KOREAN CONFLICT

Les fugitifs, feu du ciel sus les piques.

Conflict prochain des corbeaux s'esbatans,

De terre on crie aide secours celiques,

Quand pres des murs seront les combatants.

✺

Fire from above will spike the fugitives

Soon the ravens will start bickering

Earth-bound cries beg heaven for assistance

When the fighters approach the walls.

In Egyptian hieroglyphics, a 'raven' symbolises contention. In later times, it was considered a bird of ill omen, probably due to its habit of following armies and ravening on the dead bodies left in their wake. Throughout ancient history, bickerings between ravens and crows were considered as prognostications of terrible events – Jovianus Pontanus tells of such an event before the battle of Beneventum, and Nicetas speaks of a similar occurrence before the Scythians invaded Thrace. The great orator Cicero was forewarned of his death by the fluttering of ravens in his room, and the Athenian Oracle declared that 'ravens bear the characters of Saturn ... and have a very early perception of the bad disposition of that planet.'

As to the identity of the walled city in line 4, one is forced back to line 1, and the word *pique*, which can have multiple meanings. The obvious ones are 'pike', and to be 'stung' or 'spiked'. In Old French, though, a *piqué* was a quilted waistcoat, such as was traditionally worn by the Chinese or the Koreans. The word 'walls' in line 4 cements the Korean, rather than the Chinese reading, however. In the *Annals Of The Three Kingdoms*, written by Il Jon in the late thirteenth century, it is said that Tangun Wanggom set up his capital at Pyongyang Walls, and named his country Korea.

SUMMARY

North Korea will refuse to accede to the West's demands over clarification of its nuclear capacity. A crisis will be triggered which may lead to war.

ASSASSINATION AFTERMATH

5 / 8

Sera laissé feu vif, mort caché,

Dedans les globes horrible espouvantable,

De nuict à classe cité en poudre lasché

La cité à feu, l'ennemy favorable.

✻

Living fire will be unleashed, death will
be hidden

Inside frightful, terrifying globes

By night the fleet will grind the city into powder

The city on fire, the enemy ascendant.

Prediction

If the political assassination that Nostradamus predicts in quatrain 10/26 – 2006 onwards [Assassination Of A World Leader], does indeed take place, then this quatrain, with its index year of 8, shows that assassination's appalling aftermath. The action that so alienates Britain that it decides to ally itself with France (in this case symbolising the entire European Union) would appear to consist of the newly elected leader taking revenge for his brother's death against the city which spawned, or was considered to have harboured, his assassins. The irony of the quatrain, though, is that despite the overwhelming firepower of the forces involved, and the gruesomely described destruction of the unnamed city harbouring the assassins, the enemy still finds itself in the ascendant when the engagement is over. This can only mean that the unilaterally taken action contrives to alienate more people than it placates.

Summary

Following the assassination of a major world leader, the actions taken by his brother, governing in his stead, are so excessive, that traditional allies are alienated, and there is an unanticipated knock-on effect of sympathy for those held responsible for the murder.

ADVANCE WARNING OF THIRD ANTICHRIST

2010

10/10

Tasche de murdre enormes adulteres

Grand ennemi de tout le genre humain

Que sera pire qu'ayeulx, oncles ne peres

En fer, feu, eau, sanguin et inhumain.

✳

Stained with mass murder and adultery

This great enemy of humanity

Will be worse than any man before him

In steel, fire, water, bloody and monstrous.

This is an early portent of the coming of the third Antichrist, echoing the warning tones of St John The Evangelist in I John 2. xvii–xviii, even down to St John's concept of the transitory lust for material things, as postulated in 'And the world passeth away, and the lust thereof:' Nostradamus certainly doesn't pull any punches here, describing the future depredations of the Antichrist as 'worse than any man before him', which, if one considers the first two Antichrists to be either Napoleon and Hitler, or Stalin and Hitler, depending on which reading one adheres to, is really saying something. Go to 7/32 & 2/32 – 2032, 3/34 – 2034, 3/35 – 2035, 9/36 – 2036, 10/75 – 2075 and 8/77 – 2077 for a further taste of what lies in store for the next few generations.

SUMMARY

The third Antichrist will be even more destructive than his two predecessors, and the results of his actions will darken and distort the history of the twenty-first century.

GLOBAL WARMING I

5/11

Mer par solaires sevre ne passera

Ceux de Venus tiendront toute l'Affrique

Leur regne plus Saturne n'occupera

Et changera la part Asiatique.

❄

The sea, chastened by the sun, will no longer pass

The heat of Venus will harry all of Africa

Saturn will no longer measure its reign

The Asiatic part will change.

The Suez Canal will dry up due to global warming, bringing Asia closer to Africa. The heat of Venus, second planet from the sun (and the one that approaches nearest to the earth and is most similar to us in size and density) will devastate the African continent. When one considers, for a moment, that the surface temperatures of Venus are in the region of 460°, Nostradamus's image is a powerful one. Saturn appears here in the guise of Kronos (Time), with his relentless sickle to hand, the implication being that this is a permanent change – the end of a Golden Age, even – when the earth brought forth abundantly, and without the need for tilling. This reading is further reinforced by the fact that Saturn was, on the one hand, the Roman god of agriculture, and on the other, in his guise as the youngest of the Titans, the enthusiastic devourer of his own children.

SUMMARY

The effects of global warming will start to be felt in Africa, that most vulnerable of continents. There will be famine and drought, and, in some places, even cannibalism.

DANGERS TO JOHN PAUL II'S SUCCESSOR, BENEDICT XVI

4 / 11

Celui qu'aura gouvert de la grand cappe,
Sera induict à quelques cas patrer
Les douzes rouges viendront fouiller la nappe.
Soubz meutre, meutre se viendra perpetrer.

✳

He who governs with the papal cloak

Will be induced to act as shepherd

The twelve red ones will come to bury his communion cloth

Under cover of murder, murder will be done.

The Catholic Church has harboured murderers in its ranks before. Indeed, many people still continue to allege that Pope John Paul I was done away with by elements of the Curia (the Church Administration) after only thirty-four days in office, in September 1978, and that he was killed precisely because he had just completed, but not yet publicized, dismissal orders for a list of highly placed opponents of change. This time the new pope is being pushed to lead from the back, as a 'shepherd' does, by twelve massively influential cardinals. The image of the burial of the 'communion cloth' in line 3 is a worrying one, and its correlation to the 'papal cloak' in line 1 is categorical. The pope's life is definitely in danger.

SUMMARY

After a period of acting simply as the shepherd of the Church, Pope Benedict XVI decides to stretch his wings a little. There will be a threat to his life.

DEATH OF A POPE I

Esleu en Pape, d'esleu sera mocqué
Subit soudain esmeu prompt et timide
Par trop bon doulz à mourir provocqué
Crainte estainte la nuit de sa mort guide.

✻

An elected Pope, mocked by his electors

Suddenly acts, though briefly and timidly

He is killed for being too good

He will fear the death of his guide,
the night he dies.

The 'electors' in line 1 are the College of Cardinals, and not the members of the Catholic Church, who have no say whatsoever in who leads them. Uncharacteristically, and unilaterally, the pope acts, after a long period of entropy. His advisers are horrified. Though well-meaning, he is perceived to be endangering the guiding principles of Catholic dogma. On the night that he dies, the pope is already anticipating Godlessness, encapsulated in the symbolical 'death of his guide', God.

Summary

Following the threat to his life mentioned in the last quatrain, Pope Benedict XVI acts, though in an uncharacteristic manner. Either as the result of an earlier injury, or after a fresh attempt on his life, the pope dies.

PRINCESS DIANA & DODI FAYED

2012

9 / 12

Le tant d'argent de Diane et Mercure

Les simulacres au lac seront trouvez,

Le figulier cherchant argille neufve

Lui et les siens d'or seront abbrevez.

❋

Despite all the money of Diana and Mercury

Their empty shadows will be found at the lake

For the potter in search of new clay

He and his people will be drenched with gold.

Diana, Princess of Wales, and her lover, Dodi Fayed (son of Mohammed al Fayed, owner of Harrods, London's world famous department store) were killed in a car crash in Paris, early on the morning of the 31st August 1997 – a moment when neither their fame nor their fortune could help them, as Nostradamus so clearly delineates in line 1. Diana's brother, Lord Spencer, oversaw the building of a water park at their natal Althorp Estate in honour of her life, and Diana's 'empty shadow' is indeed buried on an island, on the lake, with Dodi's shadow forever bound up with hers.

Dodi Fayed is associated with Mercury, in line 1, for Mercury was the Roman god of trade, and both Dodi and his father owed their fortunes to commerce. The last two lines are more of a mystery, though. Ancient American Indian lore has it that we are all made of clay, and that Manitou simply baked the white man for too short a period, and the black man for too long a period – the red man he baked just right. This concept (with the usual variations, depending on self-interest) runs through many religions, and Romans ix. 21, is particularly succinct on the matter: 'Hath not the potter power over the clay, of the same lump to make one vessel unto honour, and another unto dishonour?'

The concept of gold inevitably leads us back to Midas, King of Phrygia, and his request to the gods that everything he touch be turned to gold. Lady Diana Spencer made a similar request by marrying Prince Charles, heir to the British throne, and so, in his way, did Dodi Fayed, when he took up with the golden-haired Diana. Perhaps the real potter Nostradamus was referring to was Demetrius, a silversmith of Ephesus, who specialised in making gold and silver shrines for the temple of Diana? When idolatry was in danger of castigation by the simplicity of the Apostle Paul's Gospel, all the silversmiths, including Demetrius, came out on strike, and, for the space of two hours (as Acts xix. 24–28 tells us) they shouted 'Great is Diana of the Ephesians!' We all know what happened next. There may be a message there, for all idolaters.

Summary

Nostradamus muses on the briefness of celebrity. Following the deaths of Princess Diana and Dodi Fayed in a car crash in 1997, all the money and fame in the world are no longer of use to them. All that remains, fifteen years on, are their empty shadows in the memorial water park at Althorp.

NUCLEAR FISSION

Par fouldre en l'arche or et argent fondu

De deux captifs l'un l'autre mangera

De la cité le plus grand estendu

Quand submergée la classe nagera.

❂

Gold and silver are fused by the ark's
devastating power

The one is cannibalised by the other

The leader of the city is stretched

When the fleet travels underwater.

The word *l'arche* has many possible connotations, ranging from alchemy (*archée*: the central fire of life), to Noah's Ark, to the Ark of the Covenant, to the concept of *être hors de l'arche* (to be beyond the pale of the Church). When twinned with the image of a 'fleet which travels underwater', we are inevitably led towards the concept of a submarine, driven by nuclear fission – an unholy power, in other words, strong enough to fuse the disparate elements of dark and light, and which threatens the security of a great city. The Ark of the Covenant, as well as being the repository of the two great tablets of the Decalogue, did, of course, also act as a safeguard in times of war, a function now taken up by the rather more secular form of the nuclear submarine. Some maintain that the Ark is now lost, but others believe that it remains under permanent guard by a single monk who never ventures into the outside world, at a remote monastic church in Ethiopia.

SUMMARY

Nostradamus compares the power of nuclear fission to that of the Ark of the Covenant, with the first bringing materialistic darkness, and the second, spiritual light.

ABORTION DEBATE REIGNITES IN THE CATHOLIC CHURCH

DATE

2013

QUATRAIN

$2/13$

Le corps sans ame plus n'estre en sacrifice

Jour de la mort mis en nativité

L'esprit divin fera l'ame felice

Voyant le verbe en son eternité.

✷

The soul-less body will no longer be sacrificed

It will be born on the day of death

The divine spirit will make the soul happy

Seeing the eternal word.

This quatrain has traditionally been taken as a straightforward hymn to the resurrection, despite the categorical nature of line 1. The 'body without a soul', however, is that of an unborn child, and not that of a human being approaching death, which already has a soul. The philosopher Aristotle taught that the unborn foetus only becomes ensouled, in the case of a male child, after forty days in the womb, and in the case of a female child, after eighty days. The Catholic Church accepted Aristotle's opinion until 1621, when its own interpretation changed to one of cross-gender ensoulment at conception, echoing, curiously enough, Buddhist views on the subject. Both St Thomas and St Jerome, though, hardliners to a man, condemned abortion outright, despite its virtual non-appearance in the Bible [Exodus xxi. 22–23, for instance, saw it only as a fining offence, except in the case of the consequent death of the mother].

The Jewish religion reflects the Old Testament view (it should be remembered that Nostradamus was a Catholic Jew, and died in 1566, before the Catholic change of tack), and holds that a child is not ensouled in the womb, but only becomes 'human' when the head appears – at this point, even if the mother is endangered, the child must not be killed. Before that, no capital offence will have occurred. This view is so widespread that, to this day, women soldiers in the Israeli Defense Forces are entitled to two free abortions during the course of their two-year stint.

What Nostradamus appears to be postulating in this quatrain, however, is that abortion is fundamentally wrong, and that the destroyed foetus is ensouled at the moment of its death ('it will be born on the day of death'), a view reinforced by the next line which reiterates the concept of ensoulment as a means of enlightenment by the divine word. The implication, therefore, is that the Catholic view of the theocratic illegality of abortion will harden, rather than soften, during the rekindling of this debate, just as it hardened back in 1621.

Summary

The abortion debate flares up again, this time within the Mother Church itself. The Church maintains its intractable line on the termination of an unborn foetus being tantamount to murder.

DEATH OF A POPE II

2014

4/14

La mort subite du premier personnage

Aura changé et mis un autre au regne

Tost, tard venu à si haut et bas aage,

Que terre et mer faudre que on la craigne.

✸

The unexpected death of the first among many

Will create change, making another man leader

Soon, but also too late, a young man will attain high office

By land and sea he must be feared.

Following on from 10/12 – 2012 [Death Of A Pope I], and 2/13 – 2013 [Abortion Debate Reignites In The Catholic Church], and anticipating the 2017 series of scandals in the Church covered in 3/17, 9/2 and 6/17, this quatrain deals with the accession of a new and younger pope to the Triple Crown. Why a pope, and not a president? Because only a pope, in the terms that Nostradamus would understand them, can be a *premier personnage*. Let us remind ourselves of what the Triple Crown represents: firstly, the Head of the Catholic, or Universal, Church; secondly, the Sole Arbiter of its rights; thirdly, the Sovereign Father of all the kings of the earth. That's pretty categorical, isn't it? The word 'fear' in line 4, should be taken, in this context, in the same way that God-fearing used to be taken, i.e. as indicating obedience, rather than terror. Given all that, we now have a relatively young pope, taking over unexpectedly from a traditionalist pope (which we know from the Abortion Debate in 2/13). The scandals predicted three years later, in 2017, are now placed in their proper perspective.

SUMMARY

A relatively young pope has acceded to the Triple Crown. He is a liberal. Following more than thirty years of largely conservative rule, his election raises hackles amongst the remaining traditionalist cardinals.

HILLARY CLINTON

2015

8/15

Vers Aquilon grans efforts par hommasse

Presque l'Europe et l'univers vexer,

Les deux eclipses mettra en tel chasse,

Et aux Pannons vie et mort renforcer.

✳

The masculine woman will exert herself to the north

She will annoy nearly all of Europe and the rest of the world

Two failures will put her in such an imbalance

That both life and death will strengthen eastern Europe.

Hillary Rodham Clinton will be sixty-eight years old in 2015, and possibly either in her first or second term as US president. If the two quatrains dealing with the assassination of a world leader and its aftermath [10/26 and 5/8 – 2006–2008], pan out as Nostradamus predicted, then by 2015 Mrs Clinton would be three quarters of the way through her first term.

During Roman times, Pannonia was a tribal area in eastern Europe bordered by Epirus in the south, and the Danube in the north, and which covers the equivalent today of much of Austria, Greece, Yugoslavia, Hungary, Albania, and even parts of Bulgaria and Turkey. Velleius Paterculus thought the Pannons untrustworthy, and Ammianus made much of their cunning and versatility. Mrs Clinton appears to annoy them.

Nostradamus's image of the 'masculine woman' obviously has nothing whatsoever to do with appearance or hormone count, but should be taken as implying a woman who takes on a job usually done by a man. In this case, trouble occurs in the northern part of Europe. The Americans, under Mrs Clinton, intervene. The same powder keg that has been exploding ever since the Pannons were a thorn in the side of their Roman masters explodes yet again, this time in response to a different form of imperialism.

SUMMARY

Hillary Clinton, having become the first ever female president of the United States, proceeds to alienate much of eastern Europe.

FAMINE RELIEF

D'où pensera faire venir famine,

De là viendra le rassasiement

L'oeil de la mer par avare canine

Pour de l'un l'autre donra huile, froment.

❋

From where they thought famine would come

Comes relief

The eyes of the sea are like a greedy dog's

One eye will provide oil, the other, wheat.

One of Nostradamus's rare optimistic quatrains, describing a famine that was thought to be about to occur, but didn't. This quatrain is of vital importance, because it casts light on where we might need to look to in the future for our resources. In a world in which the population is rapidly moving towards seven and a half billion by 2015 (the index date of this quatrain) increasing to an estimated nine billion by 2050, Nostradamus foresees the globally warming planet of the future as a place where the sea is viewed predominantly as a threat [see 1/29 – 2004: Tsunami I]. But this view is wrong, he tells us. We must instead see the oceans as fields to be tilled, and as wells to be harvested. The image of wheat conjures up a surreal image of ocean beds, seeded with grain, from which oil and bread will come. Monolithic machines, living permanently under the sea, would be needed to service such a harvest – a haunting image from a master of constructive prophecy.

SUMMARY

The world narrowly escapes a famine. Nostradamus uses this close escape to highlight the dangers inherent in an exploding world population, and exhorts us to find sustainable resources by alternative means.

ECOLOGICAL DISASTERS I

Faulx à l'estang joint vers le Sagitaire,
En son hault Auge de l'exaltation,
Peste, famine, mort de main militaire,
La siecle approche de renouvation.

❖

Scythes in the mill-run, joining towards
Sagittarius

In it high mill-course of exaltation

Plague, famine, and death through war

The century approaches its remaking.

Both *l'estang* and *auge* are milling terms, and we may assume that Nostradamus used them intentionally, to imply a grinding or milling process of ecological and alchemical change. 'Scythes', as well as implying death (a common image in fifteenth and sixteenth-century Tarot cards), would also, if taken literally, rust and become useless if thrown into a millpond. This is a direct image from the Revelation of St John the Divine 6. vi., describing the fourth of the four beasts seated before the throne of God, all of whom have eyes both before and behind them, and who are instrumental in the opening of the Seven Seals on the Day Of Wrath: 'And I heard a voice in the midst of the four beasts say, A measure of wheat for a penny, and three measures of barley for a penny; and see thou hurt not the oil and the wine.'

Sagitaire, in line 1, represents Sagittarius the archer, and he is the horseman revealed at the opening of the First Seal, by the beckoning of the first of the four beasts: 'And I saw, and behold a white horse; and he that sat on him had a bow;' [Revelations 6. ii.]. The upshot of the opening of the last of the Seven Seals is too abominable to contemplate, and we must take this quatrain as a warning, alongside its neighbours, 4/15 – 2015, 8/16 – 2016, and 1/17 – 2017, about the damage we are doing to our planet and to its climate.

SUMMARY

Another warning, by Nostradamus, of the wrong direction the world is taking

ECOLOGICAL DISASTERS II

DATE

2016

QUATRAIN

8 / 16

Au lieu que Hieron feit sa nef fabriquer,

Si grand deluge sera et si subite,

Qu'on n'aura lieu ne terres s'atacquer

L'onde monter Fesulan Olympique.

✦

In the place where Hero mourned

Such a great and sudden flood will occur

That there will be no land left to cling to

The waves will rise over Mount Olympus.

Most commentators take *Hieron*, in line 1, to be a cryptogram for Jason (of 'the Argonauts' fame), but this commentator begs to differ. It seems far more likely that Nostradamus meant Hero (in French: *Heron*), the priestess of Aphrodite who drowned herself in the Hellespont (now known as the Dardanelles) for love of Leander. Leander was from Abydos, a settlement on the opposite shore to that of Aphrodite's temple at Sestos. Each night, Leander would swim across the strait to be with his lover (just as Lord Byron swam across it many centuries later, in 1810, in honour of their love):

> *He could, perhaps, have pass'd the Hellespont,*
> *As once (a feat on which ourselves we prided)*
> *Leander, Mr Ekenhead, and I did.*
> *[Don Juan, Canto ii. St. 105]*

Hero would guide Leander towards her by the light of a torch until, one night, a great wave reared up and swept him away. Inconsolable, Hero threw herself into the sea to join him.

Nef, which the Jason camp takes, in its literal form, as 'ship', is actually an abbreviation of *néfaste*, which can mean either a 'day of mourning', or an 'unlucky, unpropitious day'. There is also a clever Nostradamian sub-plot at work here, centring on jokes. Hierocles – a cryptogram of *Hieron*, twinning both him and Hero – lived in the fifth century AD, and was a renowned jokester. He was actually the first person in recorded history to produce a collection entirely dedicated to jokes – only twenty-eight, to be sure, but everyone has to start somewhere.

The joke theme is echoed again in line 4, with the word *Fesulan*, for Fescennine Verses were lampoons, originating in Fescennia in Tuscany, aimed specifically at taking the mickey out of an unsuspecting audience. Mount Olympus (Olimbos), situated on the opposite shore of the Aegean Sea to the Dardanelles (*Cannakale Bogazi*), was the traditional home of Jupiter and his pantheon of gods, renowned, it has to be said, for their jokes, japes and pranks at the expense of mere mortals. The wave that swept Leander away was one such joke, probably perpetrated by Aphrodite, jealous that one of her priestesses should jilt her and worship instead at the shrine of earthly love. A similar wave is promised for 2016, and Nostradamus seems to feel that the gods may still be mocking us, in their own inimitable way, for our fickleness and our destructive habits in the face of god-given nature.

Summary

A massive flood is threatened in the Aegean area. It will be so catastrophic that no one on dry land will be safe.

ECOLOGICAL DISASTERS III

Par quarante ans l'Iris n'apperoistra,

Par quarante ans tous les jours sera veu

La terre aride en siccité croistra,

Et grans deluges quand sera aperceu.

✸

For forty years the iris will not appear

For a further forty, it shall be seen every day

The already arid earth will grow still more parched

Great floods, when the iris is seen again.

In Old French *l'Iris* was both a rainbow and an iris (the flower) – the first is meant metaphorically, the second literally. Iris was the goddess of the rainbow, and she is the messenger of the gods when they intend discord, the rainbow being the bridge from heaven let down for her convenience in carrying her message. The iris flower is a commonplace one, and of no special significance except in its very mundanity. Nostradamus seems to be implying that if we have reached a stage in our treatment of the planet in which such a simple organism as a flower can no longer grow, then we have reached crisis point. The last two lines are as clear a picture of global warming, followed by torrential flooding after the wholesale destruction of our moisture-holding forests, as we are ever likely to get.

SUMMARY

Our treatment of the planet is reaching crisis point. We are in danger of losing much of the natural beauty that we now take for granted. Something must be done before it is too late.

SCANDALS IN THE ROMAN CATHOLIC CHURCH I

Mont Aventine brusler nuict sera veu

Le ciel obscur tout à un coup en Flandres

Quand le monarque chassera son nepveu

Leurs gens à Eglise commettront les esclandres.

✺

Mount Aventine will be seen burning by night

The sky will unexpectedly obscure Flanders

When the leader chases out his nephew

Church people will cause scandals.

This quatrain is a prime example of the complexities involved in teasing meaning out of certain key Nostradamian quatrains. If taken literally, Mount Aventine would appear to refer to one of the Seven Hills of Rome, the hill of Aventine. However, Nostradamus (1503–1566) would also have been aware of the writings of a certain Aventinus (1477–1534), a.k.a. Johann Turmair, who originated from Abensberg, Bavaria (Latin name: Aventinum), from where he derived his pen-name, and who was the author of a famous anti-papal treatise. *Berg*, needless to say, also means 'mountain' in German. Allowing, in addition, for Nostradamus's well-known enjoyment of puns, together with the occasional eccentricities of his script, one also comes up with St Avertin, the patron saint of lunatics, so called from the French, *avertineux* (lunatics). *Avertineux*, of course, incorporates the meaning of a vertiginous, dare one say even 'mountain-like', drop, from sanity into insanity.

Added to all this, there will, indeed, be a total eclipse of the sun on 21st August 2017, the index date on the quatrain, and, remarkably, it will be visible from Flanders. At around this time, says Nostradamus, the pope will unwisely (insanely?) force a trusted cardinal/lieutenant out of office, creating a furore that will threaten the very foundations of the Church.

Summary

The pope causes a crisis in the Roman Catholic Church by forcing out the man whom many assumed would succeed him.

SCANDALS IN THE ROMAN CATHOLIC CHURCH II

Du hault du mont Aventin voix ouie,

Vuidez, vuidez de tous les deux costez,

Du sang des rouges sera l'ire assomie,

D'Arimin Prate, columna debotez.

✳

A voice is heard from high on Mount Aventine

Leave, leave, all of you, on both sides

Anger will only be satisfied if the reds bleed

The calumny is revealed by Rimini and Prato.

Following on in meaning from the previous quatrain (3/17 – 2017), this quatrain continues the theme of a damaging schism within the Roman Catholic leadership. The pope asks the opposing sides to withdraw from the debate, but the laity demand blood (an accounting) from the cardinals. The source of the original calumny is then revealed by two Italian cardinals, born in Rimini and Prato respectively.

SUMMARY

The crisis in the Roman Catholic Church deepens, and an accounting is called for by the laity.

SCANDALS IN THE ROMAN CATHOLIC CHURCH III

DATE

2017

QUATRAIN

6/17

Apres les limes brusler les aziniers

Contraints seront changer habits divers

Les Saturnins bruslez par les meusniers

Hors la plupart qui ne sera convers.

✲

After their correction has burnt the ass drivers

They will be forced out of their habits and into new clothing

The Saturnians are roasted by the millers

Though most of them will not be converted.

The index date is the giveaway here – 2017. A continuation of Nostradamus's prophecies (3/17 – 2017 and 9/2 – 2017) concerning the scandals in the Roman Catholic Church. 'Ass drivers' in line 1, is a comical euphemism for the priesthood, who will be forced to change out of their 'habits and into new clothing' – they will be defrocked, in other words. Ptolemy (Claudius Ptolemaeus), the celebrated mathematician, astronomer and geographer, said in his *Compost* (which Nostradamus would certainly have read in the normal course of his education): 'The children of the sayd *Saturne* shall be great jangeleres and chyders …and they will never forgyve tyll they be revenged of theyr quarrel.' So despite being 'put through the mill', most of the recalcitrant priests (the *Saturnians*) will refuse to back down from their entrenched positions, and may well go so far as to found a schismatic Church to counter the established Church of Rome.

SUMMARY

Seeking to avert a catastrophe, the pope defrocks a number of prominent schismatics. There is the real danger of a fundamental rift in the Roman Catholic Church if matters are not quickly brought to order.

AL-QAEDA

Les bien aisez subit seront aesmis
Par les trois freres le monde mis en trouble,
Cité marine saisiront ennemis,
Faim, feu, sang, peste et de tous maux le double.

✺

The comfortably off will lose half their possessions

The trouble comes from three brothers

Enemies will seize the naval city

Hunger, fire, blood, plague, and of every evil, the twin.

The 'three brothers' are the three fatwas, or religious rulings, issued by al-Qaeda, calling on all Muslims to take up arms against the USA ('the comfortably-off'). Al-Qaeda was founded by Osama Bin Laden during the late 1980s, to unite Sunni Arabs against religious interlopers, and was allegedly behind, amongst other things, the World Trade Center attacks in 2001 [see 1/87 and 10/49 – 2001], the bombing of the US Embassies in Nairobi and Dar Es Salaam in 1998, and the seaborne attack on the USS *Cole* in Aden, in 2000. This last may give us our clue to the naval city mentioned in line 3, which would seem to be a US naval base located somewhere near the Arab world. It should perhaps be mentioned that Osama Bin Laden was born in 1958, and will only be 59 years old in 2017.

SUMMARY

Al-Qaeda continues its policy of antagonism towards the United States. This time a US naval base is attacked, and temporarily restored to Arab control. The United States retaliates in kind.

AFTERMATH OF ROMAN CATHOLIC SCHISM

Tous les amis qu'auront tenu parti,

Par rude en lettres mis mort et saccagé,

Biens publiez par sixe (fixe) grand neanti,

Onc Romain peuple ne feut tant outragé.

❖

All the friends who held fast are now gone

Brought down and ransacked by those of little learning

The great one destroyed, his goods auctioned off

Never were the Roman people so insulted.

Three years after the schism in the Roman Catholic Church [see 3/17, 9/2, 6/17 – 2017], things are now back to something approaching normal. No one, however, has emerged unscathed from the resulting scandal. In lines 1 and 2 we read that the schismatics have finally given in, under pressure from the archconservatives. In line 3 we learn that their leader has been brought low, his reputation in tatters. The implication in line 4 is that the stemming of dissension within the Church is a tragedy for the worldwide Catholic congregation.

S U M M A R Y

The schism in the Roman Catholic Church has been healed. Old wounds still fester, however, and the danger of a backlash remains.

TERRORIST ATTACK IN SOUTHERN FRANCE

Au port d'Agde trois fustes entreront

Portant d'infect non foi et pestilence

Passant le pont mil milles embleront,

Et le pont rompre à tierce resistance.

✷

Three low-slung ships enter the port of Agde

Carrying infected unbelievers and plagues

Many things will happen, a million souls will die

The bridge will break at the third arch.

Some juicy puns, here, with four separate meanings for *pont*, as in, the bridge of a ship, much water passing under a bridge, a traditional bridge, and a metaphorical bridge. In addition, a *ponté* is a decked boat, though not dissimilar to the *fuste* mentioned in line 1, which is a thin, flat vessel. *Pont* is also an abbreviation for the pontiff, or pope. Bridges, in medieval France, were traditionally built with three arches and three towers (a good example is Pont Valentré in Cahors), and *ponte* meant both the 'laying of eggs' and the 'ace of trumps'. All this to show how rich a brew even an apparently straightforward quatrain by Nostradamus can be.

However we choose to untangle the wordplay, though, one thing is clear – the Mediterranean coast of France is in for a terrorist attack by men carrying the plague (both spiritual and biochemical) inside them. The bridge mentioned in line 4 is perhaps that of *Al Serat*, the ordeal bridge over which all Mohammedans must pass on their way to the resurrection. It is only as wide as the blade of a scimitar, and the faithful may cross over in perfect safety, while sinners will topple over the edge, into hell. It would surely not be stretching a point too far to read line 4 as Nostradamus's belief that the bringing of plague on their enemies makes of every Mohammedan who supports the act a sinner, overloading *Al Serat*, and causing it to fracture at the third arch?

SUMMARY

A terrorist attack through the French port of Agde, with suicidal extremists incubating biochemical infections.

BIRTH OF AN ISLAND

Profonde argile blanche nourrit rocher,
Qui d'un abysme istra lacticineuse
En vain troublez ne le seront toucher,
Ignorant être au fond terre argileuse.

✺

A deep white clay feeds the rock

Which boils up from an abyss like milk

Needlessly afraid, the people won't touch it

Being ignorant of the clay in the earth's heart.

The image of a 'rock boiling up like milk' brings to mind the spontaneous creation of the island of Surtsey, near the Vestmannaeyjar (Westman Islands), off the southern coast of Iceland, on November 15th 1963. This was a spectacular fire-and-brimstone birth, in which ash, pumice and cinders burst 1,000 feet into the sky, after more than six invisible months spent travelling to the ocean's surface. At times the ash column reached heights of 30,000 feet, and was visible from as far away as Reykjavik. Volcanic activity is commonplace beneath the surface of the oceans, so anticipating the location of any new arrival is difficult. But Nostradamus describes an environment here that is still relatively primitive – an environment possibly closed off to Western eyes. North Korea? The Indonesian Archipelago? Cuba?

SUMMARY

The birth of a new island, due to undersea volcanic activity, in an area of the world still off limits to the West.

PRINCE HARRY'S PATERNITY

Par le despit du Roi soustenant moindre,

Sera meurdri lui presentant les bagues,

Le pere au filz voulant noblesse poindre

Fait comme à Perse jadis feirent les Mague:

✺

Because of the King's anger, a lesser one
is sustained

He will be bruised when he is offered jewels

The father, wishing to prick his son towards
nobility

Does what the Maguses once did in Persia.

So what *did* the Maguses once do in Persia? Maguses were priests, but the particular Magus whom Nostradamus is probably referring to was Gaumata of Media. When dissolute King Cambyses (son of Cyrus the Great) left his brother Bardiya as regent while he was away at war, he almost immediately had second thoughts, and ordered his brother secretly killed, fearing that he might be tempted to usurp the throne for good – Cambyses himself then conveniently went on to die from a wound to the hip during the course of the campaign (possibly by his own hand). On hearing of Cambyses' death, the Magus Gaumata, who was in on the secret killing of Cambyses' brother, impersonated Bardiya so well that he was able to rule for a full seven months in his stead, and might have passed himself off as king for good and all if Darius and some other of Cambyses' courtiers hadn't rumbled him. Darius, who was not of the royal blood himself, went on to found his very own dynasty, and one is forced to wonder whether the whole thing wasn't a very convenient plan, hatched by the priests, to get their own man onto the throne of Persia.

Now, given the contents of 10/22 – 2022 [Abdication Of Charles III Of England], all of this becomes very relevant indeed. The implication of that quatrain is that, Prince William being out of the picture, Prince Harry becomes king in his father's stead. Thanks to the fragility of Prince Charles's marriage to Princess Diana, a certain measure of sceptical doubt has often manifested itself over Prince Harry's true paternity. *If* it were to be the case that Harry was not Charles's son, and *if* it were to be the case that a situation arose in which he were to be offered the throne, then Nostradamus's prediction would undoubtedly be proved true. The 'offering of jewels' in line 2 refers, of course, to the Crown Jewels of England (which include the two great Cullinan diamonds, and the near-mythical Koh-i-Noor), and the verb *meurtrir*, to bruise, beautifully sums up a possible crisis of conscience over a deception. The rest (as they don't say) is history.

Summary

Prince Harry takes over from Prince William as the formal successor to his father – the future King Charles III – as ruler of the United Kingdom. There is intense media speculation about Prince Harry's true paternity.

SUCCESSION TO THE UK THRONE

Par fureur faincte d'esmotion divine,

Sera la femme du grand fort violee

Juges voulans damner telle doctrine,

Victime au peuple ignorant imolee.

✳

Through the pretend fury of divine emotion

The wife of the great one will be badly wronged

Judges wish to condemn such a doctrine

The victim will be sacrificed to the ignorant people.

The future King Charles III and his Princess Consort, the former Camilla Parker Bowles, will find themselves faced with a constitutional crisis on the death of Charles's mother, Queen Elizabeth II. This crisis will be provoked by the Church of England, which is traditionally headed by the monarch. The General Synod, motivated by a desire to run its own affairs without interference from the State, will contrive the crisis based on an attack on the couple's civil wedding. Legally, the attack will be without foundation, and judgment will be found in the couple's favour, but, by using the power of the proletariat (i.e. through the media), the General Synod will get its way. The relevant index date is afforded by the next quatrain, 10/22 – 2022, which continues the prediction.

SUMMARY

A constitutional crisis occurs on the death of Queen Elizabeth II. Disestablishment of the Church of England, thanks to the civil nature of Charles's second marriage to the former Camilla Parker Bowles, is a distinct possibility.

ABDICATION OF CHARLES III OF ENGLAND

Pour ne vouloir consentir à divorce,
Qui puis apres sera cogneu indigne,
Le Roi des Isles sera chassé par force
Mis à son lieu que de roi n'aura signe.

❂

Because they disapproved of his divorce

A man, who, later, they considered unworthy

The people will force out the King of the Islands

A man will replace him who never expected
to be king.

This quatrain will come as no surprise to the British people, and it has wide implications. The first is that Queen Elizabeth II will die, circa 2022, at the age of around ninety-six, five years short of her mother's term of life. Prince Charles will be crowned in her stead, and become 'King of the Islands', the implication here being that he is no longer king of the other regions in the world over which his mother reigned – Canada, Australia, New Zealand, etc. – which will have, in the interim, become republics. Prince Charles will be seventy-four years old in 2022, when he takes over the throne, but the resentments held against him by a certain proportion of the British population, following his divorce from Diana, Princess of Wales, still persist. The pressure on him is so great, and his age so much against him, that Charles agrees to abdicate in favour of his son. The question is, which son? For in the last line Nostradamus makes it very clear that 'a man will replace him who never expected to be king'. Does this mean that Prince William, who would have expected to succeed his father, is no longer in the picture? And that Prince Harry, by process of default, becomes king in his stead? That would make him King Henry IX, aged just thirty-eight.

SUMMARY

King Charles III of England, weary at the persistent attacks on both himself and his second wife in the twenty-five years since his first wife, Princess Diana's death, decides to abdicate in favour of her son, Prince Harry.

POOR SIR BEVIS

Le camp Ascap d'Europe partira,

S'adjoignant proche de l'isle submergée

D'Arton classe phalange pliera,

Nombril du monde plus grand voix subrogée.

❁

The Ascap camp leaves Europe

Re-forming near the submerged island

The d'Arton fleet folds and bends

A new world centre, with a louder voice,
replaces it.

Commentators love this quatrain as it is so infinitely amenable and full of happy wordplays, like *Ascap* and *d'Arton*, affording seemingly endless vistas of speculative possibility, twinned with not a little innocent amusement. Most leap on the 'Nato' for *d'Arton* bandwagon, while others concentrate on the *Ascap/Ascop* Greek dimension, which gives us 'aimless' or 'imprudent'. *Camp*, too, is a juicy conundrum, and can be construed as meaning anything from an 'army', through a 'scholars' holiday', to a 'plumped-up domestic fowl'. It can also, of course, mean 'camp'.

This commentator's guess is that Nostradamus has split *Ascap* and *partira* on purpose, to disguise the identity of Ascapart, the thirty-foot giant (he had a twelve-inch gap between both eyes) who conquered Sir Bevis of Southampton and carried both him, his wife, and his horse off underneath one arm [see Shakespeare's *Henry VI Part Two*, act ii. 3]. Originally known as *Boeve d'Haumtone*, this well-known thirteenth-century Anglo-Norman *chanson de geste* went through many transmogrifications, *à la* Don Quixote, and was still much read in Nostradamus's time. The United Kingdom connection is further reinforced by Nostradamus's customary use of the 'submerged island' image for the British Isles, and given the index date, which closely matches that of 1/21 – 2021 [Birth Of An Island], and the series of quatrains about the British royal family contained in 10/21, 6/72, and in particular 10/22, in which the island image reoccurs, it seems foolhardy to assume that they are not, in some way, connected.

It's devilishly tempting, too, to look for a misspelling in the word *d'Arton*, giving us *Daron*, which, in Old French, was a sobriquet given to shopkeepers – for this would lead us towards the delightful image of Samuel Adams's 'nation of shopkeepers' (i.e. the British) taking to the sea in a decidedly leaky boat. If readers feel that the Samuel Adams connection is a remotely tenable one, then the final line leads us neatly back to the United States, in the temporary guise of the monster Ascapart, taking over from Britain as the dominant world power. Where this leaves poor Sir Bevis of Southampton, though, is anybody's guess.

Summary

Nostradamus casts his eye over the new great imperial power, the United States, and compares it with the old imperial power it eventually took over from, Great Britain. His comparison is not complimentary to the United States.

NEW FIRST FAMILY – PRECURSOR

Les deux contens seront unis ensemble

Quand la pluspart à Mars seront conjoinct

Le grand d'Affrique en effrayeur et tremble

Duumvirat par la classe desjoinct.

❋

The two contenders will unite together

When most others unite with Mars

The African leader is fearful, and trembles

The dual alliance is separated by the fleet.

This seems to be a precursor to 6/24 – 2024 [New First Family], both in its use of the word *conjoint*, its concentration on dualism (*Duumvirat*), and its emphasis on the link with Mars. It seems that a false alliance is undertaken, although both sides, curiously, have made the connection in good faith. 6/24 has the alliance as that between a strong man and a weak, or even a male and a female leader. That said, the alliance does not, in fact, break up, but out of havoc brings appeasement – an appeasement which is, by its very nature, only a temporary alleviation of a fundamental problem.

SUMMARY

Two great powers unite together in order to combat a global increase in internecine warfare. The alliance is a curious one, and works almost despite itself. Its good effects will not be long lasting, however.

NEW FIRST FAMILY

Mars et le sceptre se trouvera conjoinct,

Dessoubz Cancer calamiteuse guerre

Un peu apres sera nouveau Roi oingt,

Qui par long temps pacifiera la terre.

❖

Mars and the sceptre are like husband and wife

Under Cancer there will be a calamitous war

Soon afterwards a new King will be anointed

Who, for a long time, will appease the earth.

Nothing is quite as it seems in this quatrain. *Conjoint* does not simply mean joined, as most commentators would have it, but in Old, as opposed to Modern French, it implies a husband and wife, or an established common-law couple. Now here, all of a sudden, we find warlike Mars married to the virginal Sceptre, symbol of sovereignty and control, and most probably a reference to Agamemnon's famous sceptre, originally forged by Vulcan, and revered for its capacity to produce miracles.

Cancer, the crab, is famous for having bitten Hercules on the foot during his battle with the Hydra – before it had time to scuttle away, however, it was squished by the mighty one. Juno (who had sent the hapless crustacean after Hercules in the first place) took pity on the crumpled beast, and dispatched it to heaven, where it was made one of the twelve signs of the zodiac. So are Mars, Hercules, Agamemnon's Sceptre, and Cancer some kind of hidden code? This commentator's guess is that the Mars-like Agamemnon is the key, a man who sacrificed his own daughter, Iphigenia, to appease the goddess Diana and guarantee fair winds for the Greek fleet on their way to Troy. Clytemnestra, Agamemnon's adulterous wife, later slew him in his bath, and was killed, in her turn, by their son, Orestes. Just your normal, everyday, First Family.

S U M M A R Y

The alliance between the two great powers, mentioned in the last quatrain, will continue. One will sacrifice the other, leaving only one leader to appease the world.

SUNNI/SHIITE WAR

Le prince Arabe Mars, Sol, Venus, Lyon

Regne d'Eglise par mer succombera

Devers la Perse bien pres d'un million

Bisance, Egypte, ver. serp. invadera.

❖

The Arab prince Mars, the Sun, Venus and the Lion

The reign of the Church will be vanquished at sea

Close to a million men will head towards Persia,

Byzantium, Egypt, the followers of the true serpent will invade.

This is a complex quatrain to untangle, and it would seem wiser, for reasons that one trusts will become obvious, to start at the end. The phrase 'followers of the true serpent' defines any class, dogma or religion that seeks to undermine Christianity – in this case Nostradamus would appear to be talking of the Arabs (ergo Muslims). Christian iconography persistently translates the serpent into either Satan, or the Tempter, and he is usually pictured crushed underfoot by St Cecilia, St Euphemia, or, thanks to the promise made to Eve after the Fall ['And I will put enmity between thee and the woman, and between thy seed and her seed; it shall bruise thy head, and thou shalt bruise his heel.' Gen. iii. 15.], he finds himself placed beneath the feet of the Virgin.

Now we go back to line 1, and the Arab prince and his attributes. Mars, as we know, is the alchemical symbol for iron, the Sun for gold, and Venus for copper [see 4/28 – 2028: Discovery Of The Philosopher's Stone], and all of these metals are presumably transmuted, as we see from line 1, into human characteristics. The Lion, as ultimate benefactor of these transmutations, is the traditional agnomen accorded to a succession of great Arab leaders, amongst whom we find Ali, cousin and son-in-law of Muhammad, whose mother called him Al Haïdara, or the Rugged Lion, at his birth; Alp Abslan, the son of Togrul Beg, the Perso-Turkish monarch, who was known as the Valiant Lion; Ali Pasha, who was known as the Lion of Janina before his overthrow by Ibrahim Pasha in 1822; and Hamza, Muhammad's uncle, known as the 'Lion Of God And Of His

Prophet' after his arrival in heaven. So it seems, at first glance, that we are dealing here with a religious war, or lesser jihad. But the million strong army mentioned in line 3 is heading *towards*, and not away, from Arab lands. Could we then be talking of a Sunni/Shiite rift?

The Sunnis, who constitute the majority of the Arab world, have traditionally regarded Shiism as verging on the heretical, while the Shiites, who make up approximately ten percent of the remainder, see themselves as representing the purist strand of Islam. Nostradamus, from both his Catholic and his Jewish perspective, would of course view both strands of Islam as equally snaky.

Summary

The rift between Sunni and Shiite deepens, leading to war.

SIX LUCKY GAMBLERS

Dedans les isles de cinq fleuves à un,

Par le croissant du grand Chyren Selin

Par les bruines de l'aer fureur de l'un,

Six eschapés, cachés fardeaux de lin.

※

In the islands where five rivers flow into one

By the crescent of the great Chyren Selin

The fury of one man will float on the mist

Six will escape, hidden in a load of linen.

The 'great Chyren Selin' has appeared in one guise or another, in eleven other Nostradamian quatrains, and he presents us with something of a problem. The crescent mentioned here gives us a clue, though, and points to an Islamic connection, as the Sultan Othman, founder of the great Turkish Empire (Ottoman), allegedly had a vision of a crescent moon spreading its horns from east to west, and later took it as his standard – the crescent still appears on the Turkish flag to this day. The moon connection is heightened by the word *Selin*, for Selene was the fecund moon-goddess who rode through the heavens on a chariot drawn by two white horses, and had more than fifty daughters.

Chyren is often taken as a cryptogram for Henry, but he may more sensibly be equated with Charon (pronounced Chyren), the boatman of the River Styx, who required payment, in the form of a penny, to ferry dead souls across to Hades. Charon was also the personification of the darkness of the earth, which brings us back, once again, to the crescent moon, which throws but little light.

All that said, we are left with 'the islands where five rivers flow into one'. This may be taken not only geographically, but also metaphorically, as five, or the *pentad*, is the great mystic number, and represents the unity of God alone (without creation). The fact that 'six will escape' also has significance, as the number six means everything or nothing, and referred, in Greek and Roman times, to the random throw of three dice.

In our painfully literal modern-day world, it might be tempting to discount all the previous clues, and simply take the quatrain as it stands. That would be a mistake. If 'five' is the great mystic number, and it flows into 'one' (God), then Chyren Selin is the ferryman, embodiment of the darkness that awaits us before the resurrection – for Hades was not hell, of course, but rather an antechamber to either Erebus (the darkness before the light of Paradise) or Tartarus (that part of the infernal regions where the wicked are punished). The 'six that escape, hidden in a load of linen', refers back to the habit of burying the dead in a linen shroud, and one might be tempted to infer that these six escapees were gambling men, who tricked the furious Charon out of his coin (and the customary one-hundred-year penalty for those who did not pay his toll), and snuck in beneath the wire, just like Alexandre Dumas's Count Of Monte Cristo did, during his escape from the Chateau D'If.

Summary

Punjab, in Hindi, means 'five rivers', and it is conceivable that Nostradamus is speaking of a war between India and Pakistan, as parts of the Punjab lie in both countries. The quatrain remains a resolutely personal one, though, and more than a little opaque.

DISCOVERY OF THE PHILOSOPHER'S STONE

DATE

2028

QUATRAIN

4 / 28

Lors que Venus du Sol sera couvert,

Soubs l'esplendeur sera forme occulte

Mercure au feu les aura descouvert,

Par bruit bellique sera mis à l'insulte.

❇

When Venus is covered by the Sun

Shapes will be concealed beneath its splendour

Mercury, with its fire, will expose them

They will be misused in war.

In Olympiodorus's *Meteorologica*, Venus was associated with copper, the Sun with gold, and the planet Mercury (Hermes) with mercury. All are alchemical totems. We are dealing, therefore, with the transmutation of metals (mercury into gold, say), a theory devised by the ancient Greeks and elaborated by the Arab and Latin alchemists who followed them. This was a search for the *prima materia* (prime matter, or the soul of mercury), and we know, from Nostradamus's mention of philosophical mercury and its 'fire' (which was thought to consist of sulphur, or its hybrid, the Philosopher's Stone) that he believes it will be discovered around this date.

This seems strange, as Nostradamus must have read Paracelsus during his medical studies (which he completed in 1529, a bare three years after Paracelsus had achieved his widest fame), and been aware of Paracelsus's opinion that the true object of alchemy was not the making of gold, but rather the preparation of medicines and the clarification of the homeopathic principle. Be that as it may, Nostradamus declares here that the Philosopher's Stone will definitely be discovered, and that it will subsequently be misused in warfare. Given the advanced state of chemical science in the twenty-first century, who dares gainsay him?

SUMMARY

Nostradamus is probably describing the first use of cloned human beings in conventional warfare.

FINANCIAL
MELTDOWN

Les simulacres d'or et argent enflez,

Qu'apres le rapt au lac furent gettez

Au desouvert estaincts tous et troublez.

Au marbre script prescript intergetez.

✺

Fake versions of gold and silver multiply

After the abduction they are thrown into the lake

On their rediscovery, global exhaustion and trouble.

All debts are voided.

A global financial meltdown in 2028, triggered by the use of artificial replacements for cash – i.e. credit cards, national debt, and a raft of other financial instruments? As well as abduction, *rapt* can also be used in the sense of a 'rape'. Following the rape of the financial markets, therefore, and the worldwide collapse of fake monetary objects, all debts between nation states are voided. Whether this will also apply to individual debt is a touch more debatable. See 2/28 – 2028 [Religious Revival] for an alternative reading.

SUMMARY

It is the one hundredth year after the great 1929 Wall Street stock market crash, and Nostradamus is predicting another, similar event. This time, the crash will mirror the collapse of spiritual values throughout the Western world.

RELIGIOUS REVIVAL

Le penultiesme du surnom du prophete,

Prendra Diane pour son jour et repos

Loing vaguera par frenetique teste,

Et delivrant un grand peuple d'impos.

✲

The last but one holder of the prophet's name

Will take Diana for his day and for his rest

He will wander far with his head in a frenzy

Delivering a great people from financial subjugation.

This quatrain is particularly interesting given its index date link with 8/28 – 2028 [Financial Meltdown]. Both deal, quite clearly, with taxes, debt, and financial crisis, but this one has a spiritual dimension as well, and forces us back to a second possible reading of 8/28, in which 'fake versions of gold and silver' become false religious icons. The Koran claims that there have been 200,000 prophets, but that only six are significant, in that they have brought in new laws and dispensations. These six are Adam, Noah, Abraham, Moses, Jesus and Muhammad. A prophet is, technically speaking, one who announces the divine will, and stems originally from Ancient Greek, although the meaning is strictly Hebrew. The Hebrews themselves recognized many prophets, and the Gautama Buddha, of course, would also come under this category, though he encapsulated the Light, rather than merely interpreting it. Nostradamus, though a scryer and seer, would certainly not have considered himself amongst their number, however.

The Roman goddess Diana's day is Monday, as she took over, amongst other things, the post of goddess of the moon from the Greek goddess Artemis. The Roman habit of filching things from the Greeks rather muddies the water where Diana is concerned, but she was also supposed to promote the union of communities, and to represent plebeians and slaves. In France Saint Lunedi was the saint associated with Mondays, and it became, in consequence, a day of rest for workers, further cementing the links in the first two lines of the quatrain. Although this does not bring us much closer to the identity of the 'last but one holder of the prophet's name', it does lead us very nicely into 2/29 – 2029 [The Sun I], which is most probably what Nostradamus intended.

Summary

Following the great financial crash of 2028, a spiritual vacuum can be detected throughout Western society. There is a gradual return to organized religion.

THE SUN I

L'Oriental sortira de son siege,

Passer les monts Apennins voir la Gaule

Transpercera le ciel les eaux et neige,

Et un chacun frappera de sa gaule.

❂

The man from the East will leave his home

And cross the Apennine Mountains, to see France

He will pierce through the skies, the seas, and the snow

He will strike everyone with his staff.

The sun rises in the east (at least we hope so), and people are buried with their feet towards the east to show that they died in the hope of resurrection. We turn to the east when saying the Creed, and even the Greeks insisted that their cadavers should lie face upwards, and with their feet pointed towards Elysium – well away from the inferno in the west, in other words, and the sinister regions of the night. The east, then, is a powerful concept, and the place towards which we customarily look for enlightenment. All this to say that Nostradamus was most probably alluding to the sun, when he spoke of the 'man from the east', and if one reads the quatrain in that way, it is actually rather beautiful.

Another reading would judge the 'enlightenment' from the east metaphorically, as spiritual enlightenment. Here the concept of the 'staff' comes in, with its revocations of the ancient sceptre, which traditionally meant power, authority and dignity. Kings, of course, struck chosen recipients with their staff to raise them high in the realm, and to 'strike one's staff' also meant to lodge somewhere for the night, with the staff, in this instance, implying a tent-staff. This brings us neatly back to the sun, and to its role in creating a suitable environment in which to grow bread – a.k.a. the 'staff of life'. So perhaps this is a prayer?

SUMMARY

The return to spiritual values foreseen in the last quatrain is reinforced in this hymn to the abundance of the sun, and to enlightenment.

THE SUN II

Le Sol caché eclipse par Mercure,

Ne sera mis que pour le ciel second

De Vulcan Hermes sera faicte pasture,

Sol sera veu pur, rutilant et blond.

✳

The sun is hidden, eclipsed by Mercury

It will take second place in the sky

Hermes will be eaten by Vulcan

The sun will be seen, pure, gleaming, and fair.

This time we are dealing, not with a prayer, but with an invocation. An invocation to change. The image of Mercury is the key, with its revocations of alchemy and the transformation of base metals – we know, of course, that tiny Mercury (which is about the same size as the earth, and is the nearest planet to the sun), would not be capable of eclipsing the sun *except* in metaphor. So the sun is temporarily eclipsed by the power of mankind.

However, Hermes (the Greek Mercury, and in this case the symbol of the onward thrust of mankind's scientific discovery) proves to have been, quite literally, playing with fire, for he finds himself eaten, in his turn, by Vulcan, the blacksmith, whose dominion fire is (as it was of Hephaestus, with whom he is often identified). The sun, in the guise of Apollo, the great moral champion, is not so easily cowed by human actions, though, and soon shows Hephaestus who is the real boss of fire, as Milton describes in *Paradise Lost*, Book 1, from line 742 onwards:

> *Sheer o'er the crystal battlements: from morn*
> *To noon he fell, from noon to dewy eve,*
> *A summer's day, and with the setting sun*
> *Dropt from the zenith, like a falling star.*

So this is a warning, then, after the elucidatory prayer of thanks in the previous quatrain – a warning not to tinker with things greater than ourselves, and which we don't fully understand [see 4/28 – 2028: Discovery Of The Philosopher's

Stone]. Icarus, son of the talented but elusive Daedalus (himself a descendant of Hephaestus), thought that he, too, could challenge the sun, and look what happened to him. The wax on his man-made wings melted, and he fell into the Aegean Sea, part of which, as a sop, was named in his memory.

Summary

Nostradamus warns of the seductive dangers of science, at the expense of morality and right-thinking. This quatrain is a paean to philosophy.

POLITICAL CORRECTNESS I

Es lieux et temps chair un poisson donra lieu

La loi commune sera faicte au contraire

Vieux tiendra fort plus osté du millieu

Le Pánta chiona phìlòn mis fort arriere.

✸

A time will come when meat gives way to fish

Communal law will go against the people

The old order will fight hard and then be ousted

The will of the people will be repulsed.

Meat will be banned. Vegetarianism will be enforced through the common law. Despite a valiant rearguard action by the old guard (unregenerate libertarians?) the State will succeed in imposing its will on the people. Many otherwise liberal states are already heading in this direction, with restrictions on the smoking of tobacco and on free speech, amongst other things. The picture Nostradamus conjures up for us is far worse, however, and if his predictions prove true, George Orwell's *1984* will have come that little bit closer.

SUMMARY

A warning of the dangers of woolly thinking, and the loss of our capacity to discriminate for fear of offending others. This will lead to the downfall of democracy under the false guise of inclusion.

BIRTH OF THE THIRD ANTICHRIST – PRESAGE I

2032

7/32

Du mont Royal naistra d'une casane,

Qui cave, et compte viendra tyranniser

Dresser copie de la marche Millane,

Favene, Florence d'or et gens espuiser.

✦

Though born in poverty, he will take supreme power

He will tyrannise and bankrupt his people

Raising a thousand-year army

Though lucky, he costs lives and gold.

This is a presage to the great quatrain number 3/35 – 2035 [Birth Of The Third Antichrist]. Nostradamus often plays these games, referring back to earlier quatrains whose meaning he was unsure of at the time. There is much wordplay in this one, which would allow for two separate readings. However, if we acknowledge the wordplay, and do not take *Millane*, *Favene* and *Florence* as literally meaning 'Milan', 'Faenza' and 'Florence', we come up with *mille ans* for *Millane* ('a thousand years'), *sa veine* for *Faveine* ('his luck'), and 'gold florins' for *Florence d'or*. Place names were rarely fixed in Nostradamus, and were often capitalized to draw attention to themselves and to the secrets hidden inside them, as with his use of the word *Hister*, for example, in the famous Hitler quatrains presaging the Second World War (Hitler was most probably the second Antichrist). *Hister* can also mean the Danube, near which Hitler was born, and also hysteria, from which Hitler undoubtedly suffered. The source of the word comes from the ancient Greek, *hustérā*, meaning womb, thus reinforcing the concept of a birth.

SUMMARY

The third Antichrist will soon be born. His birth will be a disaster for the world.

BIRTH OF THE THIRD ANTICHRIST – PRESAGE II

2 0 3 2

2 / 3 2

Laict, sang grenouilles escoudre en Dalmatie

Conflict donné, peste pres de Balennes

Cri sera grand par toute Esclavonie

Lors naistra monstre pres et dedans Ravenne.

❁

Milk and the blood of frogs flows in Dalmatia

Battle is joined, there is plague near Balennes

Wailing will echo throughout enslaved Slovenia

When the monster is born in and near Ravenna.

The second of three presages to quatrain number 3/35 – 2035 [Birth Of The Third Antichrist] contains a rather nice reference to one of Aesop's fables. A frog and a mouse decide to engage in single combat to settle the question of who owns the marsh they both live in. With the battle well under way, and their attention concentrated elsewhere, an artful kite swoops down unexpectedly and carries both combatants off. Ancient 'Dalmatia' lies almost entirely inside modern-day Croatia, which has traditionally been fought over by the Serbs and the Croats [see 9/60 – 2060: Serbo-Croatian Conflict] – it hardly stretches the imagination, therefore, to imagine the Serbs as frogs and the Croats as mice, and the Muslim minority, or perhaps even the Russians, as the artful kite? Either way, battle is joined near *Balennes* (which is probably Baleni Romini, in Romania, situated forty miles north of Bucharest).

The monster, or third Antichrist, is then born in, or near, Ravenna. It may, at this point, be apposite to point out that as well as the more obvious Ravenna, in Italy, there are also two Ravennas in the country formerly known as Yugoslavia. One, Ravna Reka, is in Serbia, and the other, Ravne na Koroskem, is in Slovenia, which ties in quite nicely with line 3.

S U M M A R Y
The three possible sites of the third Antichrist's birth are given. Bad luck will come to those countries abutting the place.

US PRESIDENTIAL ELECTION

QUATRAIN

10/32

Le grand empire chacun an devoir estre

Un sur les autres le viendra obtenir

Mais peu de temps sera son regne et estre

Deux ans aux naves se pourra soustenir.

❋

The great empire will continue, year on year

One man will snatch it from the others

Both his life and his reign will be brief

He will only carry the load for two years.

This is a non-specific quatrain about duty, and about *estre*, or 'being' (the s having been replaced by a circumflex in modern French), with the key word, *naves*, occurring in line 4. *Navée* means 'a large load', and the man who snatches control of the empire – which in this case can only mean the United States, the last great empire left on earth – finds the burden a heavy one, and will remain in office for only half a term as president. Whether this means that he is impeached, or dies, is not made entirely clear, although line 3 appears to incline us towards the latter.

S U M M A R Y

A US president finds the weight of high office too much for him, and succumbs under the strain. He only manages to complete half his term.

CLASS WAR

Par Fraude regne, forces expolier,

La classe obsesse, passages à l'espie

Deux fainctz amis se viendront rallier,

Esveiller haine de long temps assoupie.

❂

Trickery will reign, the army will be stripped

An obsession with class, spying given free rein

False friends will unite

Hatred, once quiescent, will be reawakened.

Following on in date from 4/32 – 2032 [Political Correctness I], this quatrain describes a time in which class divisions are rekindled, in which Big Brother is watching us with a less than fraternal attention, and in which the army – the sometime final protection against State tyranny – is stripped of its powers through fraud and trickery. Alliances will be contrived, not to say expedient, and will be driven, not by a sense of political duty, but by hate. Individuals will be encouraged to spy on each other, to denounce their neighbour, and even to conduct witch hunts, just as happened in the notoriously illiberal period running up to the Second World War, in Spain under General Franco, in Germany under Adolf Hitler, in Russia under Joseph Stalin, and in France under Maréchal Pétain. All these regimes were obsessed with class, and purported to be governing on behalf of the so-called proletariat while in fact they were busy promulgating their very own forms of plutocracy.

SUMMARY

Class warfare will be rekindled under the guise of social inclusion. The army will be fatally weakened. Politicians will wield too much power. A reaction will set in.

POLITICAL CORRECTNESS II

En grand regret sera la gent Gauloise

Coeur vain, legier croirera temerité

Pain, sel, ne vin, eaue: venin ne cervoise

Plus grand captif, faim, froit, necessité.

❖

The French nation will be consumed by regret

With a frivolous heart, they trusted to rashness

Bread, salt, no wine, water; poison, not beer

Their leader made captive: hunger, cold, and want ensue.

Moving directly on from 4/32 – 2032 [Political Correctness I], and from 7/33 – 2033 [Class War], this quatrain continues the theme of enforced vegetarianism and alcoholic prohibition in a country previously renowned for its progressive tolerance of all the diverse strands of human behaviour – i.e. France. Wine and beer are banned, and meat, once the staple of an enlightened French cuisine, has given way to fish (as we know from 4/32). The leader of the old guard, who obviously fights a valiant rearguard action against the illiberal restrictions, is imprisoned. Catastrophe ensues.

SUMMARY

The historical lessons about prohibiting others from doing what they enjoy have not been learned. Politicians, wielding greater than usual power, abuse it. People, deprived of their pleasures, and lacking joy, lose heart.

POLITICAL CORRECTNESS III

L'ire insensee du combat furieux

Fera à table par freres le fer luire

Les despartir, blessée, curieux

Le fier duelle viendra en France nuire.

✦

The senseless anger of the furious war

Will cause brothers to unsheathe their knives
across the table

Driven apart, wounded, prying

The pride-driven duel will hurt France.

Civil unrest has now come to France, as a result of the increasingly demented strictures of the European superstate [see 7/34 – 2034: Political Correctness II]. The French people, never ones to allow themselves to be controlled by laws they despise, are forced into a virtual civil war, where brother fights brother 'across the table'. The 'across the table' image also contains within itself a sneaking reference to the banning of meat and game, for which, in peasant France, the near-ubiquitous knife would be used, in, amongst other things, the bleeding of rabbits [see 4/32 – 2032: Political Correctness I].

'Prying', in line 3, is a direct reference to 'spying' in line 2 of 7/33 – 2033 [Class War], and to the rekindling by the State of a situation last encountered during the Second World War under the Pétainiste government of unoccupied Vichy France, when informing on one's neighbour was positively encouraged.

Summary

The French finally rebel against the evils of political correctness and spoilsport politics. The great traditions of the barricade, and the proletariat fight for freedom, are reawakened.

BIRTH OF THE THIRD ANTICHRIST – PRESAGE III

2034

3 / 3 4

Quand le deffaut du Soleil lors sera.

Sur le plain jour le monstre sera veu

Tout autrement on l'interpretera,

Cherté n'a garde mil n'y aura pourveu.

❁

At the total eclipse of the sun

The monster will be seen in broad daylight

He will be misinterpreted

None will have foreseen the great cost.

In 2034 a total eclipse of the sun is expected on the 20th March, a little ahead of the sun's transit from Pisces into Aries, the sign of wars, famines, heat, droughts, and magical transformation. The eclipse will pass over central Africa, the Middle East (including Egypt and Iran), and south Asia (including India and China). It will presage the birth of the third Antichrist [3/35 – 2035], and he will be conceived in the period immediately following the eclipse, and born in the new year. We know that this is a significant presage because of the paradox hidden within the quatrain, namely that 'at the total eclipse of the sun' (i.e. when all is darkness), 'the monster will be seen in *broad daylight*'. We also know from 2/32 – 2032 that the monster (from the Latin *monstrum* meaning not only a prodigy, or monster, but also an omen, or scourge) will be born either in Italy, Serbia, or Slovenia, all areas well outside the line of the eclipse. His coming will be welcomed by many with secret vested interests, but it will ultimately portend disaster.

SUMMARY

The third Antichrist is conceived, in darkness, during the total eclipse. He will be born into darkness, too, and he will bring darkness upon the world.

WINTER FREEZE

8 / 35

Dedans l'entrée de Garonne et Baise

Et la forest non loing de Damazan

Du Marsaves gelees, puis gresle et bize

Dordonnois gelle par erreur de Mezan.

✷

At the entrance to the Garonne and Bazas

And the forest close to Damazan

Mont-de-Marsan is frozen, then hail and
northerly winds

Dordogne freezes, but in the wrong house
(Mézin).

The geographical location of this great frost is absolutely specific, and earlier commentators appear to have missed that *Baise* is Bazan, *Mezan* is Mézin, and *Marsaves* is the Mont-de-Marsan. All the places mentioned are geographically located within a forty-mile radius of each other, on the south bank of the River Garonne, in south-western France, and Nostradamus, as usual, is enjoying his puns, with *Mezan* and *maison* (house) neatly juxtaposed. The Dordogne (situated sixty miles to the north) is renowned for its abominable winter weather, with temperatures of as low as -15°C not uncommon, and Nostradamus implies here that, in this particular winter of 2035, the usual freeze happens in the wrong place.

SUMMARY

A terrible winter freeze will hit the towns and villages on the south bank of the Garonne river. The people will not be expecting it. It will catch them catastrophically unprepared.

BIRTH OF THE THIRD ANTICHRIST

Du plus profond de l'Occident d'Europe

De pauvres gens un jeune enfant naistra

Qui par sa langue seduira grande troupe,

Son bruit au regne d'Orient plus croistra.

❄

From deep in the Western part of Europe

A child will be born, to poor parents

He will seduce the multitude with his tongue

The noise of his reputation will grow in the
Eastern kingdom.

This new leader of the Muslim world will be around thirty-five years old by the time of the Global War referred to in quatrain number 5/70 – 2070. Though only from a humble background in the western Islamic diaspora, he will manage to pull together the equivalent of the old Ottoman Empire by the seductive power of his language, and threaten the dominant positions of the US and China. This will result in a catastrophic nuclear war, 'powerful enough to disturb mountains' [see 5/70]. The worrying aspect of this quatrain lies in the word *seduira*, 'to seduce' or 'deceive by charm', in line 3, with its implication that this leader will be a manipulator and a fixer, and also in the word *bruit*, in line 4, implying that his reputation will be spun as a form of narrative, rather than fairly earned. It's a worrying quatrain in every respect, and echoes the presage of Adolf Hitler, as the possible second Antichrist, in the now famous quatrain 2/24:

> *Bestes farouches de faim fleuves tranner,*
> *Plus part du champ encontre Hister sera.*
> *En caige de fer le grand fera treisner,*
> *Quand rien enfant de Germain observera.*

> With the hunger of wild beasts they cross rivers
> Most of the world will be against Hister
> The great man will find himself inside a cage of
>   iron
> The German child understands nothing.

This is the closest Nostradamus ever came to a warning to the future world, and the subtle language he uses in 3/35 – 2035 echoes this, with its hints of hidden depths and secret manipulations.

SUMMARY

The third Antichrist is born. The die has been cast. The future of the world, unless a miracle occurs, will be very bleak, with global warfare and ecological damage on an unprecedented scale.

BIRTH OF THE THIRD ANTICHRIST – CONSEQUENCES

DATE

2036

QUATRAIN

9/36

Un grand Roi prins entre les mains d'un Joine,

Non loing de Pasque confusion coup coultre

Perpet. captifs temps que fouldre en la husne,

Lorsque trois freres se blesseront et meutre.

❊

A great King falls into the hands of a youngster

There is confusion around Easter time, and a knife-blow

Long-term captives, and St Elmo's Fire

When three brothers wound and kill each other.

This is not the only time that Nostradamus uses the image of St Elmo's Fire [see 2/90 – 2090: Hungary In Crisis]. He has also used the concept of 'three brothers' before, particularly in 8/46 – 2005 [Death Of Pope John Paul II]. In that quatrain the 'three brothers' symbolised the Magi, and, given the Easter motif in this quatrain, there is no reason to suppose that he is not using the same trope once again. One's instinct is to connect this quatrain with that of the preceding year, 3/35 – 2035 [Birth Of The Third Antichrist], and if that is the case, Nostradamus is giving us a second warning. The 'child born to poor parents' is most definitely *not* the Second Coming, as, in his case, the Magi (figuratively) fall out. The mention of 'Easter time' is an obvious reference to the death of Christ, and this is further strengthened by the mention of a 'knife-blow', which equates with the lance driven into Jesus' side. Given all this, it would appear that the 'great King' in line I refers directly to Jesus, and that it is He, or more correctly his followers, who risk falling into the hands of 'the youngster', causing confusion.

SUMMARY

The third Antichrist will be declared the Second Coming. This will not be true. He will damage both the world and the Christian Church.

WAR BETWEEN AUSTRALIA & INDONESIA

EARLY 2037

1/37

Un peu devant que le soleil s'excuse,
Conflict donné grand peuple dubiteux
Profliges, port marin ne faict response,
Pont et sepulchre en deux estranges lieux.

❈

Shortly before the eclipse of the sun

A war is triggered by a great nation of unbelievers

Wastefully, the seaport does not fight back

Bridge and memorial are dissevered.

The total solar eclipse of 13th July 2037 virtually splits Australia in two, from north to south, exiting between Sydney and Brisbane to finish up over the South Island of New Zealand. Australia is the 'great nation of unbelievers' (secular state) therefore, and the war Nostradamus predicts is started by them.

When we turn to the three clues Nostradamus gives us about the nation it attacks, 'the seaport', 'the bridge', and 'the memorial', we find ourselves inexorably drawn towards Surabaya, the second largest city and seaport in Indonesia after Jakarta's Tangung Priok, and home to more than three million people. Surabaya's largest monument, Tugu Pahlawan, is a memorial to the heroes who died during Indonesia's struggle for independence from 1945 to 1949, and the famous Red Bridge (Jembatan Merah), now known as China Town, is the site of the Great Battle of Surabaya, which took place on 10th November 1945.

SUMMARY

Indonesia and Australia fall out over supremacy in the Indian Ocean. The dispute snowballs into armed conflict, followed by all-out war.

REVERSAL OF AGEING PROCESS

L'oeuvre ancienne se parachevera,

Du toict cherra sur la grand mal ruyne,

Innocent faict mort on accusera,

Nocent cache, taillis à la bruyne.

❋

The ancient work will be completed

From the cherished roof, ruin will fall on the evil leader

An innocent dead man will be accused

Hidden by darkness, the guilty one runs away into the drizzling rain.

This quatrain would appear to be about alchemy, a word which stems from the Arabic *al kímía*, and means the secret art. Its objects were threefold, and accorded with the three great secrets of science, namely to transmute base metals into gold, to create the universal solvent, and to discover the elixir of immortal life. But alchemy was about more than simply mechanical transmutation and the chemistry of the middle ages – it also had a strong philosophical basis, handed down from the ancient Greeks, and which has served to unify chemical effort into the empirical science it is today. Nostradamus was an alchemist and a Kabbalist, of course, as well as being a physician, and elements of the Science of Angels, which claimed to provide a key to the universe and to raise the individual soul to the ecstasy of mystical contemplation, would have been synonymous with his natural mode of thought.

Given all this, what are we to make of the quatrain? Are we to accept that the secrets of immortality have been broached? Or does it simply mean that, through the magic of DNA, we have succeeded in slowing down the ageing process? Either way, the secret is being abused.

SUMMARY

Medical science has made great strides towards reversing the natural depredations of age. These advances are accepted without qualm. Nostradamus warns us that they will have evil consequences if they are not sufficiently thought through.

GRAECO/TURKISH PROBLEM

Les Rhodians demanderont secours
Par le neglect de ses hors delaissée
L'Empire Arabe revalera son secours
Par Hesperies la cause redressée.

❋

The people of Rhodes will ask for help

Robbed, thanks to the actions of their forebears

The Arab Empire returns like for like

Its cause is straightened out by the West.

PREDICTION

The island of Rhodes lies about as near to the Turkish
mainland as one can get without actually becoming a part of
it, and even a cursory glance at a map of the Aegean area will
afford one an unsettling insight into some of the causes of
the ancient antagonism between Turkey and Greece. It's all
too intimate by half down there, and the powder keg looks
set to blow again. A fair partition, in Turkish terms, would
give them Rhodes, Kos, Samos, Lesbos and Khios, etc., and
probably Ikaria too. Assuming, for a moment, that Turkey is
now in the EU, some accommodation may one day have to
be made, just as it has been made on Cyprus [see 3/89 – 2089:
Cyprus Partition]. Given the increasing dependence on Arab
oil by the Western economies, enlightened pragmatism may
well be the name of the game here.

SUMMARY

The ancient antagonism between the Greeks and the Turks
over national boundaries rekindles. The rift is so great that
independent arbitration is called for.

GREAT STORM

Un peus apres non point longue intervalle

Par mer et terre sera faict grand tumulte

Beaucoup plus grande sera pugne navalle,

Feux, animaux, qui feront plus d'insulte.

❋

A short while after a previous occurrence

A further fierce storm will rise over land and sea

The sea-borne cost of this one will be even larger

Fire, animals, it will be an even greater outrage.

A double whammy. One storm hidden by another. Already reeling from the depredations of one great storm, the world will not be prepared for a second, even greater one. For a description of the effects of such a storm, one has only to go back to Nostradamus's Tsunami I prediction, in 1/29 – 2004, or forward to his future Tsunami predictions in 4/80 – 2080 and 5/81 – 2081.

SUMMARY

Just as the world is recovering from one great storm, another, worse storm, follows. Communities are taken by surprise. Existing damage is compounded.

END OF MONARCHY IN BRITAIN I

Le jeune nay au regne Britannique,

Qu'aura le pere mourant recommandé,

Icelui mort Lonole donra topique,

Et à son fils le regne demandé.

✳

The young man, born to rule Britain

Though commended by his dying father

Once the father is dead, London will cavil

And the kingdom will be taken back from his son.

Following on from 6/72 – 2022 [Succession To The UK Throne] and 10/22 – 2022 [Abdication Of Charles III Of England], this is a particularly difficult quatrain to call. King Henry IX (the former Prince Harry) would be around fifty-six years old by this date, and would have reigned for close on eighteen years. One might reasonably assume that any son of his might be in his twenties, by 2040, thus 'the young man, born to rule England' mentioned in line 1. Nostradamus, though, makes it clear that, despite the dying King Henry commending his son to the nation, following the age-old tradition, as their new monarch – London, or in this case, the will of the people, won't have it. One is forced to assume, therefore, that Nostradamus is predicting the end of the British monarchy.

S U M M A R Y

Twelve hundred and ten years after King Egbert was first pronounced *Bretwalda* (Ruler of the British), the United Kingdom finally loses her monarchy.

END OF MONARCHY IN BRITAIN II

2040

4/40

Les fortresses des assiegés serrés
Par poudre à feu profondés en abisme
Les prodireurs seront tous vifs serrés
Onc aux sacristes n'advint si piteux scisme.

❋

The castles of the besieged will be locked

They will fall because of gunpowder

The traitors will be imprisoned alive

Never before have the Saxons been so piteously
divided.

This is a certain follow-on to 10/40 – 2040 [End Of Monarchy In Britain I]. We know this because Nostradamus scatters a series of clues throughout the quatrain. Firstly the castles traditionally associated with the royal family – Windsor, Buckingham Palace, Balmoral, etc. – will be annexed and locked up. Secondly, the royal house will fall because of 'gunpowder' [see line 2], echoing the famous Gunpowder Plot of the 5th November 1605 against James I, originated by Robert Catesby, and in which Guy Fawkes – later to join Joan of Arc as one of the two most famous bonfire victims in history – volunteered to set off the gunpowder.

As a monarchist himself, Nostradamus did not approve of plots against either kings or the established State, and his image, in line 3, of the traitors carrying their own imprisonment (guilt) within them, confirms that position. Line 4 is self-evident, the implication being that the British have made a grievous mistake in ridding themselves of the monarchy that has traditionally held them together as a nation, and that divisions will increase, rather than diminish, as a result.

SUMMARY

Nostradamus predicts that with the fall of its monarchy, Britain will lose the cement that bound it together as a nation.

END OF MONARCHY
IN BRITAIN III

2040

5/40

Le sang royal sera si tresmeslé,

Contrainct seront Gaulois de l'Hesperie

On attendra que terme soit coulé,

Et que memoire de la voix soit perie.

✳

Royal blood will be diluted

France will be gagged by the Americans

Some time will need to pass

Until the memory of all that was said passes
away.

The third of this trio of quatrains, all dealing with the British royal family and republicanism, and all categorically linked by their index dates [see 10/40 and 4/40 – 2040]. Hesperus (Venus) is the evening star, and is the first to appear in the western skies after the setting of the sun. The Greeks called Italy Hesperia, because to them it seemed the westernmost land. The Romans, needless to say, gave the name to Spain. For us, of course, the westernmost lands are the Americas.

Venus (Hesperus) was also the goddess of love and courtship, and there is an obvious link here with line 1, in which royal blood is seen to be diluted. Could there have been a birth out of wedlock, throwing the British succession into disarray? This might tie in with France needing to be 'gagged by the Americans', because, according to the European Constitution, a bastard child would need to be seen to have exactly the same rights as a child born inside a regularized marriage, something that does not tie in with British royal protocols. The schism between Britain and France is obviously a deep one, if the Americans are required to come in and act as referees.

SUMMARY

Republican France rejoices at the end of the British monarchy. Republican America is less triumphal, and attempts to rein France in.

BIRTH OF PAN-AFRICAN LEADER

DATE

2041

QUATRAIN

5/41

Nay souz les umbres et journée nocturne
Sera en rege et bonté souveraine
Fera renaistre son sang de l'antique urne,
Renouvellant siecle d'or pour l'aerain.

✻

Born inside the shadows, on the very day
of an eclipse

He will be sovereign in rule and goodness

He will renew his blood at the ancient urn

Restoring the golden age with bronze.

After the traumas suffered by the British royal family in 10/40, 4/40 and 5/40 – 2040, it would be nice to be able to report that a child was born to them who would rekindle a renewed respect for the monarchy. However the total eclipse Nostradamus mentions in line 1 covers Angola, the Congo, Uganda, Kenya, and Somalia, and not western Europe, so it is of a Pan-African leader that we are talking here. This reading is further strengthened by the expression 'ancient urn' in line 3, for we now know that Africa, and in particular the geographical areas comprised within Kenya and Tanzania, was, in all probability, the cradle of human life.

'Bronze', too, has its role to play in this reading, as it was one of the earliest known alloys, and is cast on a bed of clay. The strong implication in line 4, then, is that we need to revert back to the simplicities and certainties of the past in order to be able to renew the future, and that the great African leader Nostradamus speaks of will achieve this miracle.

This is a deeply optimistic quatrain, and very comforting in the light of the horrors awaiting humanity in the next fifty years. Perhaps Africa, wisely led for a change, will be able to hold itself apart from the world conflict, and present itself as an agent for renewal at a time of global upheaval?

SUMMARY

A great African leader is born. He will unite traditionally disparate tribes and countries.

RELIGIOUS WARS I

2043

4 / 43

Seront ouys au ceil les armes battre

Celuy an mesme les divins ennemis,

Voudront Loix Sainctes injustement debatre,

Par foudre et guerre bien croyants a mort mis.

❁

Weapons of war will scream in the sky

That same year even holy men will become enemies

They will unfairly attempt to suppress the Sacred Law

True believers will die by war and shock.

The 'Sacred Law' is probably the Ten Commandments, which in Nostradamus's time was also a euphemism for the scratching of the face with ten fingers, in the case of a woman, or the smashing action of two male fists, in that of a man. Shakespeare was conversant with the concept too, and used the image in *Henry VI Part Two*, act i. 3: 'Could I come near your beauty with my nails, I'd set my ten commandments in your face.' Sir Walter Scott uses a similar metaphor in *Waverley*, so it was not simply a Shakespearean trope. It could, however, also be applied to the Sharia, or Sacred Law of Islam, the amalgam of four otherwise disparate schools of Sunni thought comprising the Koran, the *sunna*, the *ijma*, and the *qiyas*.

The term 'true believer' also tends towards the Islamic definition. Shiites, who form a minority of approximately ten per cent within the Islamic world, believe in their own set of 'sacred laws', handed down by infallible *imams*, lineal descendants from the Prophet Mohammed's cousin and son-in-law, fourth caliph Ali ibn Abi Taleb. Their traditional stronghold is in the Islamic Republic of Iran, with smaller, minority outposts, in Iraq and Lebanon. When all this is taken into account, there is the strong possibility that, in 2043, we could be facing another Iran/Iraq war. The last one, which lasted from 1980 to 1988, resulted in more than a million casualties.

SUMMARY

A new Iran/Iraq war is in the offing, placing Shia against Sunni. There will be many casualties.

RELIGIOUS WARS II

2 / 43

Durant l'estoille chevelue apparente,
Les trois grans princes seront faits enemis
Frappés du ciel paix terre tremulante,
Pau, Timbre undans, serpent sus le bort mis.

✳

When the shooting star appears

The three great princes will fall out

World peace will falter, struck from the sky

Both Tiber and Po will overflow, and a serpent
will be placed on their banks.

There will be two great meteor outbursts from long-period comet dust trails during 2043 – the first will occur on the 31st March, at 21.36 GMT, and the second on the 22nd November at 10.58 GMT. Following on from the Religious Wars of 4/43 – 2043, the three great world leaders of Russia, China and the United States, will fall out over the correct way to respond to the crisis. 'Serpents', although traditionally understood to represent Satan (in Hindu mythology, Hell is called Narac, the region of serpents), were also considered symbols of renovation and regeneration, and it was long assumed that they were capable, when old, of growing young again, by sloughing their timeworn skin between two rocks. Rivers, also, were seen as regenerative, and this allows us to read the last line in the quatrain as fundamentally optimistic, at least in the short term.

SUMMARY

World powers fall out over the correct way to respond to the Iran/Iraq war. The schism, though deep, is eventually papered over. The patching will be temporary.

CHEMICAL WARFARE

2044

6 / 44

De nuict par Nantes L'Iris apparoistra,

Des artz marins susciteront la pluie

Arabique goulfre grand classe parfondra,

Un monstre en Saxe naistra d'ours et truie.

✵

A rainbow will appear, by night, near Nantes

Seafaring men will call up artificial rain

A great fleet will be fused in the Arabian gulf

In Saxony, a monster will be born of a bear and a sow.

This quatrain must be approached metaphorically, as much as literally. First we have Iris, in line 1, goddess of the rainbow, but also the messenger of the gods when they intend to sow discord. Why Nantes? Perhaps because it is a major port, and a manufacturing centre of chemicals, which would tie in with the creation of seeded, or 'artificial', rain. The word *parfondre* is a tricky one, and no longer used in modern French. In Old French it means to fuse, or melt together, and was much used in alchemy, and in the making of enamel. In this context it could mean both melted, in its literal sense, and destroyed, in its metaphorical sense, as mechanical objects that are fused together can no longer, by definition, function.

Saxony is an ancient region in north-western Europe, upon which Charlemagne imposed Christianity in 772 AD – it is now part of a reunified Germany. The 'bear' almost always refers to Russia, but it also means 'independence', as in Dryden's 'The Hind And The Panther':

> *The bloody bear, an independent beast,*
> *Unlicked to form, in groans her hate expressed.*

The concept of the 'sow' meant that someone had got hold of the wrong vessel (a sow was a tub, with handles), as in 'You have got hold of the wrong sow by the ear' – the 'bear' and the 'sow' are also inimical, one being independent and free, the other being domesticated. Given all this, it would seem that the quatrain foretells a time when chemical warfare is again on the agenda, and that Nostradamus feels that this is very wrong. A 'monster' is born by the fusing of disparate elements that were never meant to be united, and this will sow discord, as exemplified by the appearance of the goddess Iris over the French factory that manufactures these articles.

Summary

Great strides are made, in secret, in the realm of chemical warfare. Nostradamus warns that the genie must not be let out of the bottle.

CATHOLIC/JEWISH MISCEGENATION

Trop le ciel pleure l'Androgyn procrée,
Pres de ciel sang humain respondu
Par mort trop tard grand peup'e recrée,
Tard et tost vient le secours attendu.

❖

How heaven mourns the birth of the Hermaphrodite

Near to heaven, human blooc is shed

Too late, through death, a great people are recreated

Help comes both too early, and too late

The 'monster, born of a bear and a sow' mentioned in 6/44 – 2044 [Chemical Warfare], is echoed here, a year later, in the birth of the 'hermaphrodite'. Hermaphroditus was the son of Hermes and Aphrodite. He was so beautiful that the nymph Salmacis (whose name was later given to a fountain in Caria which turned all those who bathed in it effeminate), fell passionately in love with him, and prayed to the gods that they might become one. The gods, with their rather robust sense of humour, took her at her word, and the two became united in one body.

Ancient French law, in a rather uncharacteristic fit of tolerance, acknowledged the existence of hermaphrodites, and allowed them considerable latitude, and the Jews too, through the Talmud, gave them special privileges – such forbearance, though, probably refers back to Genesis i. 27 and Genesis ii. 20–24, and to God's creation of woman from Adam's rib, rather than to any more enlightened motivation. In other cultures, in particular that of ancient Athens, hermaphrodites were put to death as unnatural, while the Hindus and the Chinese insisted that the hermaphrodite choose one sex, and then stick to it willy-nilly.

Given the context, it is at least possible that Nostradamus is mourning an 'unnatural' mating of two sexes into one, possibly as a result of human interference – if this is indeed the case, then a reference back to the Chemical Warfare discussed in 6/44 – 2044 is the most likely source of the 'bear/sow' miscegenation. But perhaps he is talking of his own fusing of Catholic and Jew? In that case the 'recreation of a great people, through death' that he mentions in line 3, might refer specifically to the Jews, and Nostradamus might be foreseeing (a long shot, this, but feasible) the creation of the State of Israel on the back of the Holocaust? If that is the case, then an index date of 1945, rather than 2045 would be more apposite, allowing a three-year leeway between the true revelation of the extent of the Holocaust in 1945, and the foundation of the State of Israel (*Medinat Yisra'el*) in 1948.

SUMMARY
A warning that unnatural mixtures, either chemical or human, rarely work.

COLLECTIVE UNCONSCIOUS

Apres grand troche humaine plus grand s'appreste,

Le grand moteur des Siecles renouvelle

Pluie, sang, laict, famine, fer et peste,

Au ciel veu feu, courant long estincelle.

❖

Following one great human tragedy, a greater
lies in wait

The mighty movement of the centuries
brings renewal

Rain, blood, milk, famine, sword and the plague

Fire will be seen in the sky, with a trail of sparks.

In its renewal theme, this quatrain harks back to 2/43 – 2043 [Religious Wars II], but the renewal in question seems Dionysiac, rather than Apollonian (*pace* Nietzsche's *Birth Of Tragedy*) – violent and visceral, that is, rather than gradual and germane. Yet another link to 2/43 comes in the 'shooting star' image, and one sometimes wonders whether, in a sort of spontaneous morphology, the accrued wisdom of past ages isn't transmitted down the centuries in the form of unconscious remembrance, as promulgated in Jung's concept of the collective unconscious, or even the Akashic records. This would explain, too, why humanity persists in viewing the arrival of comets, meteors, asteroids, and shooting stars, etc., as harbingers of change, or precursors of apocalyptic events. If we have a collective unconscious memory of past strikes and their aftermaths, then it is hardly surprising that, when faced with the possibility of an extra-terrestrial impact, we anticipate, and even promulgate, dynamic change.

SUMMARY

There will a restlessness throughout the earth as people prepare, intuitively, for the coming of a great catastrophe. Signs will be sought, and auguries looked for.

METEOR STRIKES AS HARBINGERS OF CHANGE

DATE

2046

QUATRAIN

1/46

Tout aupres d'Auch, de Lectoure et Mirande,
Grande feu du ciel en trois nuits tombera,
Chose adviendra bien stupende et mirande,
Bien peu après al terre tremblera.

✦

In the vicinity of Auch, Lectoure and Mirande

A great fire will fall from the sky for three nights

A stupendous, well-aimed, and spectacular
occurrence

Soon afterwards the earth will tremble
and be ruffled.

Once again we find that quatrain index dates are linked in meaning across different Nostradamian *Centuries*. This time 1/46 shares the image of a 'great fire falling from the sky' with its near twin, 2/46 – 2046 [Collective Unconscious], which gives us 'fire will be seen in the sky'. This quatrain, too, uses pun and wordplay to deflect our attention from a more literal reading of the text. To *mire* in Old French, is to aim a gun, and *al terre* in line 4 contains the double meaning of 'all the world' and to be 'ruffled', or 'irritated'.

Nostradamus would have known the towns of Auch, Lectoure and Mirande very well from his period of residence in Agen, in the Gers. It was there, of course, that he lost his first wife and their two children to the plague, so the place would have had mixed memories for him, of both past happiness and present grief. All the more reason then to look beyond the literal to a spiritual renewal, brought about by a physical cataclysm. For Nostradamus, the physical cataclysm would have been the death of his family, the trauma of which helped to trigger his prophetic powers. For the earth to change, and to discover its own hidden resources, Nostradamus anticipates the need for a greater – dare one say even communal – cataclysm.

SUMMARY

Some see global catastrophe as the essential trigger needed for fundamental spiritual change, while others fear the onslaught of uncertainty.

ELECTION OF A POPE

2046

5 / 46

Par chapeaux rouges querelles et nouveaux schismes

Quand on aura esleu le Sabinois

On produira contre lui grans sophismes,

Et sera Rome lesse par Albanois.

❋

The cardinals will find new reasons to
quarrel and bicker

When the Sabine is elected

Sophistry will be used against him

And Rome will be led by the nose by
an Albanian.

More internecine rivalries within the Catholic Church. This time, the College of Cardinals decide to elect an Italian, from Rome itself, to head the Church (the Sabines traditionally lived in the mountainous country to the east of the River Tiber, and were involved in the founding of Rome). If one were to continue on in a south-easterly direction, of course, from the country of the Sabines, one would eventually arrive in Albania, from where the 'joker in the pack' of this quatrain hails.

SUMMARY

An Italian pope is elected, but elements within the Curia contest the election, and undermine it from within.

MAFIOSI KILLING I

Lac Trasmenien portera tesmoignage
Des conjurez serez dedans Perouse
Un despolle contrefera le sage
Truant Tedesque de sterne et minuse.

❁

Lake Trasimeno will show

That the conspirators are to be found in Perugia

A despot will imitate a sage

Killing the German through the breastbone
and face.

A secret is discovered in Lake Trasimeno (situated only a few miles from Perugia), which throws light on a murder committed previously, on a German. *Des conjurez* means 'those who have sworn an oath', and we know that, in Italy, the Cosa Nostra requires such a blood oath from all its members. Founded in the thirteenth century as a secret society, the Mafia remains a powerful force in southern Italian society to this day, so Nostradamus's inspired 'a despot will imitate a sage' image, probably applies to a publicity-hungry Mafia leader who grabs the high moral ground without having earned it, possibly as a result of a prominent court case.

Summary

A high-profile Mafia killing garners headlines. *A Capo di Tutti Capi* (Mafia boss of bosses) makes the most of his day in court.

MAFIOSI KILLING II

2047

I / 47

Du Lac Lemans les sermons fasceront,

Des jours seront reduit par des sepmains,

Puis mois, puis an, puis tous dafaliront,

Les Magistrats damneront leurs loix vaines.

✹

Oaths will be taken on Lake Leman

Days will become weeks

Then months, then a year: all will default

Magistrates will curse their useless laws.

Curious, the use of 'lakes' in this quatrain, 1/47, and also in its twin, 8/47 – 2047 [Mafiosi Killing I]. Knowing what we do of Nostradamus, there is almost bound to be a connection. *Tedesque*, in line 4 of 8/47, nominally means a German (from the Old French *Tudesque*, or Teutonic), but can also mean a German speaker, or speaker of *Schwyzertütsch* (Swiss German), an Alemannic language.

The two quatrains are also joined by the concept of oaths, and the dual meaning of *sepmains*, in line 2, which can mean both a week, and the bringing together of seven hands in the forming, let's say, of a secret society (Cosa Nostra). The number 'seven', as we remember from 5/81 – 2081 [Tsunami III], is a holy number, but it can also encompass the seven deadly sins of Pride, Wrath, Envy, Lust, Gluttony, Avarice, and Sloth – all notable adjuncts of the criminal classes. The number seven is also used indefinitely, to signify a long time – Shakespeare talks of a man being 'a vile thief this seven year'. Given all this, it seems that we are presented with a mysterious death, in these two quatrains, and the inability of the authorities either to catch, or to have condemned, the miscreants who perpetrated it.

SUMMARY

Interpol are powerless in the face of the *omertà* (silence in the face of the authorities) promulgated by Mafia members. The murderers of the prominent German are never caught.

GLOBAL WARMING II

Plannure, Ausonne fertille, spacieuse,

Produira tahons si tant de sauterelles:

Clarté solaire deviendra nubileuse,

Ronger tout, grand peste venir d'elles.

❋

The scorching of the wide, fertile plains
of Bordeaux

Will produce so many gadflies and locusts

That sunlight will become opaque

They will devour everything, bringing a
terrible plague.

The word *planure* is Old French for the burning of wood shavings, and implies a relentless, dry heat, such as is commonly found in Africa just before the onset of a locust attack. Nostradamus's description of the wide, fertile plains of Bordeaux purposefully plays up the distinction between the traditional plenty of Europe, and the relative poverty of the African savannah. Things are set to change, however, unless we are more careful in how we treat our planet. The wine harvest, symbol of European civilization since Roman times, will be decimated, and we shall have brought a plague on all our houses.

SUMMARY

Dry winds, more commonly seen in desert regions, will strike the European mainland, devastating the wine harvest.

US HURRICANES/ GLOBAL WARMING III

La grand cité d'occean maritime

Environnee de maretz en cristal

Dans le solstice hyemal et la prime

Sera tempté de vent espouvantal.

❋

The great maritime ocean city

Surrounded by salt marshes

In both the winter solstice and the spring

Will be tormented by a frightful wind.

The fallout from 4/48 – 2048 [Global Warming II] will continue all the way from the coming of spring until the winter solstice, which occurs on or around December 21st. Ocean City is situated in Worcester County, Maryland, one hundred miles from the Annapolis Naval Academy, and surrounded by the Sinepuxent and Assateague salt marshes. Norfolk, Virginia, which boasts one of the world's largest concentrations of naval installations, combining seaports, naval bases, training schools, and dockyards, is a bare one hundred miles to the south. The area is already renowned for the severity of its Atlantic gales, and the two hurricanes which hit the area in March/April and December 2048 will be real lulus, conjured up by a rapidly warming planet.

SUMMARY

An area on the US Atlantic coast will be devastated by twin hurricanes. Important naval installations will be affected.

FRENCH IMMIGRATION

2049

3/49

Regne Gaulois tu seras bien changé

En lieu estrange est translaté l'empire

En autres moeurs et lois seras rangé

Roan, et Chartres te feront bien du pire.

❋

French State, you will be changed

Your realm will be modified in singular ways

Rouen will be eaten by other laws and customs

Chartres will be even worse.

Ever since the revolution of 1789, France has considered itself a secular state. This secularism is now challenged by the ever increasing pressure of immigrants, who claim the right to be judged, not by the laws of their adopted country, but by those of the countries and cultures they have nominally left behind. Nostradamus sees this as a threat, and indulges in the vocative case as a clear warning to his country of the threat involved. It should be remembered that Nostradamus came from a family of assimilated Jews, and it is likely that he would have felt strongly on the subject of integration for this reason. The State, in Nostradamus's view, should be more important than the individual. To that extent he was a Confucian, and the idea that immigrants should stand upon their rights and insist on being judged by different laws to that of the host country which welcomed them would have been an anathema to him.

SUMMARY

Uncontrolled immigration is starting to impact on the traditionally tolerant French way of life. Minority groups assert their right to be judged by the laws of the country of their origin, rather than by those of their host state.

TERRORISM

Contre les rouges sectes se banderont,

Feu, eau, fer, corde par paix se minera,

Au point mourir, ceux qui machineront,

Fors un que monde surtout ruinera.

❈

They will unite against the red sects

The peace will be undermined by fire, water, and iron

The plotters will die by the sword

Except one, whom the people will destroy.

PREDICTION

Red is the colour of magic. In Roman times it denoted war, and a call to arms. Even in the Royal Navy, the hoisting of a red flag indicated that no quarter would be asked for, or given. Since 1791, in France, red has also been the symbol of insurrection and terrorism, of radicalism and anarchy. Nostradamus sees nations uniting against the terrorists, who use every possible method to undermine the peace. When you die by the sword, you die by your own hand. These terrorists consider themselves martyrs, and are prepared to die for their cause – all save one, whom the crowd despatch before he is able to trigger the explosives he is carrying on his person.

SUMMARY

Terrorism is on the increase, threatening the democratic stability of a number of European states. Civil populations belatedly retaliate.

EMANCIPATION OF MUSLIM WOMEN

En cité obsesse aux murs hommes et femmes,

Ennemis hors le chef prest à soi rendre

Vent sera fort encontre les gendarmes,

Chassez seront par chaux, poussiere, et cendre.

✸

A city obsessed by walls between the sexes

Finds the enemy outside and its chief priest prepared to surrender

The wind will fan the sparks

They will be driven off by heat, dust, and cinders.

This is a fascinating quatrain, and not at all easy to read, given the double meanings in each line. The key, curiously enough, comes in line 3, with the word *gendarmes*. The traditional meaning would seem to be 'men-at-arms', or 'policemen' – in Old French, however, *gendarmes* can also mean 'sparks from a wood fire'. Once we realize this, it becomes clear that each line contains a single key word, with two quite separate meanings attached to it. In line 2 we have *prest*, meaning both 'priest' and 'prepared', and in line 1 *obsesse*, meaning both 'obsessed' and 'besieged'. In line 4 *chaux* can mean both 'lime' (used for breaking down dead bodies), and 'heat'. Nothing, it seems, is to be taken too literally.

A translation, with the alternative meanings in place, is revealed above. It's meaning is only too clear, especially when taken with 9/51 – 2051 [Terrorism]. A Muslim city, run by Taliban priests, which is both a seat of terrorism and a place where men and women are rigorously segregated, is besieged by pro-Western forces. The city is burnt, with the burning acting in a purifying capacity. One can only assume that following its purification (its liming), an emancipation of sorts follows.

SUMMARY

The downfall of a Muslim city and of a priestly class. This leads to a liberalization of certain religious laws dealing with the relations between men and women, and with women's place in a fundamentalist Islamic society.

BATTLE OF THE SEXES

2053

5/53

La loi du Sol, et Venus contendens,
Appropriant l'esprit de prophetie
Ne l'un ne l'autre ne seront entendus,
Par Sol tiendra la loy du grand Messie.

✳

The laws of the Sun and of Venus will clash

Appropriating the spirit of prophecy

Neither the one nor the other will be heard

The Great Messiah's law will prevail through
the Sun.

It is very clear, through the twinning of Apollo, god of the sun, and Venus, goddess of love, that we are dealing with a male/female equation here. As well as being the god of light, Apollo also rules over flocks and pastures and is the source of the male nomadic tradition and attraction to the wilderness, whereas Venus, goddess of gardens, epitomizes the female urge towards domestication. Apollo's laws (which are those that eventually prevail, according to Nostradamus), encourage fair play and moral excellence, while discouraging vengeance. Venus's laws encourage courtship, and chastity, and are protective, rather than creative. Nostradamus appears to be describing the dangers of an over-feminization of culture, not in a pejorative way, it needs to be added, but as a stifle to creativity, perhaps in the guise of over-regulation and political correctness [see 4/32 – 2032 & 7/34 – 2034].

S U M M A R Y

Nostradamus puts the ancient male/female equation of risk versus caution under the microscope, and predicts that risk will eventually have to win the day if society is to progress in any direction other than sideways.

BOOK BURNING

Le Neron jeune dans les trois cheminées

Fera de paiges vifs pour ardoir getter,

Heureux qui loing sera de telz menees,

Trois de son sang le feront mort guetter.

❋

The young Nero, using three chimneys

Will burn the living word in his ardour

Happy the person far from such practices

Three of his own blood will watch him die.

Part of a trio of quatrains [see also 4/52 – 2052: Emancipation Of Muslim Women and 2/54 – 2054: Monsoon Rains] which deal with the restrictive practices put into place by a fundamentalist Muslim State. The number three also arises twice within the quatrain, and is thus significant. Pythagoras considered it the perfect number, expressive of a beginning, a middle, and an end.

In this case we are dealing with the burning of books deemed blasphemous by the mullahs. Nero was a leader intimately associated with fire, who may or may not, as Roman Emperor, have ordered the burning of Rome. At the very least, or so it is alleged, he forbade the putting out of the fire, because he 'wanted to see how Troy would look when it was in flames'. But a 'Nero' is also a generic term for any bloody-minded man, relentless tyrant, or evildoer of extraordinary savagery. Could this young Nero be the now twenty-one-year-old man Nostradamus speaks of in 7/32 – 2032 [Birth Of The Third Antichrist – Presage I]? If so the number three would exactly describe his life, and its effect, for as we know from the Bible, 'the enemies of man are threefold – the world, the flesh and the devil'.

The quatrain, too, is in three stages – the 'young' Nero, with his three chimneys; the 'mature' Nero, who burns books; and the 'dead' Nero, killed by 'three of his own blood'. There are, of course, three Antichrists, too. Napoleon/Stalin, Hitler, and the strangely persuasive gentleman whose birth is announced in 3/35 – 2035 [Birth Of The Third Antichrist].

Summary

This is a plea against censorship, and in favour of freedom. The third Antichrist is building his power base by playing on his followers' greed for power over others, just as Adolf Hitler manipulated his followers through the gift of favours and of political and civic office.

MONSOON RAINS

Par gent estrange, et Romains lointaine

Leur grand cité apres eaue fort troublée

Fille sans trop different domaine

Prins chef, ferreure n'avoir este riblée.

❖

Foreigners, far from Rome

Their great city will be damaged by rainfall

A girl from not that far away

Is taken by their leader, her old bonds
still in place.

The key to this quatrain lies in the concept of 'far from Rome', which implies a Muslim city (as far from Roman Catholicism as one can get), damaged by torrential rainfall, possibly as a result of the global warming Nostradamus predicts in 4/48 – 2048 [Global Warming II]. The capture of the girl is more obscure, and may simply be a symbolical reference to a generalised loss of freedom, particularly given the reference to 'old bonds'. Another reading, though, would have the girl representing Muslim womanhood, and the 'old bonds still in place' would then refer to the restrictions placed upon females in a traditional Islamic society, restrictions which would be redoubled following a crisis.

SUMMARY

Emergency powers are triggered by a terrible flood. These are later misused in order to control and limit the freedoms of women in a traditionalist society.

US/CHINESE STANDOFF

Deux revoltes faicte du maling falcigere,
De regne et siecles faict permutation
Le mobil signe à son endroit si ingere,
Aux deux egaux et d'inclination.

✦

Two revolutions, thanks to the cunning
scythe-bearer

Kingdoms will alter in the new century

Libra will move into its house

And both sides are well balanced.

The key to both the date and the meaning of this quatrain is the mobile sign of Libra – even the placing of the quatrain, as number fifty-four in Nostradamus's first cycle of one hundred, sets it at the fulcrum, or point of balance, of the century. In astrological terms, Libra comes at a time, between the 22nd September and the 22nd October, when both day and night, if weighed, would be found to be in balance. Saturn, of course, is the 'scythe-bearer' and devourer of all his children, save Jupiter (air), Neptune (water) and Pluto (the grave) – in his other guise as Kronos (time), he cannot, of course, consume *them*. Thus the two opposing sides, America and China, will find themselves equally balanced. The world will be split between day and night, and east and west, and neither side will be able to consume the other.

SUMMARY

China and the United States are now equally powerful and equally influential on the world stage. A treaty is agreed, defusing potential areas of conflict. There is a temporary standoff.

US/CHINESE FALSE DAWN

Les malheureuses nopces celebreront

En grand joye mais la fin malheureuse

Mary et mere nore desdaigneront

Le Phybe mort et nore plus piteuse.

❋

They will celebrate the unfortunate wedding

With great joy, but it will have an unhappy end

Husband and mother will scorn the new bride

With Phoebus dead, the north has an even
worse fate.

We know from Nostradamus's tone, and his use of the classical allusion to Phoebus, that he does not mean us to take this quatrain literally. This is a symbolical wedding, and given the content of 1/54 – 2054 [US/Chinese Standoff], it is reasonable to suppose that the 'unfortunate wedding' is that between the US and China, a thesis further strengthened by Nostradamus's pun on the word *nore* in line 4, meaning both 'daughter-in-law', 'black', and 'the north'. Phoebus, the sun god, rises in the east, of course, and sinks in the west, and the word Phoebus itself comes from the Greek word *phao*, to shine. Should the sun stop shining, therefore, the world would be plunged into darkness, which, in this case, would appear to be the darkness of war.

SUMMARY

The pact between the United States and China remains fragile. Nostradamus warns of what will happen if the pact should ever fail.

ISLAM DISTURBS THE BALANCE OF WORLD POWER I

Soubs l'opposite climat Babylonique,
Grand sera de sang effusion
Que terre et mer, air, ciel sera inique,
Sectes, faim, regnes, pestes, confusion.

❋

In the reverse of a Babylonian climate

There will be much bloodshed

Land, sea, air and heaven will be iniquitous

Sects, hunger, new kingdoms, plagues and confusion follow.

A prelude to 1/56 – 2056, this is a generalised build-up to a tense situation, where the world teeters on the brink of global war, a war that we know will in fact not occur until 2070. The concept of the 'reverse of a Babylonian climate' is an interesting one, though. Babylon means 'the gate of God', but the city had already lost its position of importance well before the rise of Islam in the seventh century AD – even Alexander the Great died before he was able to make it the capital of his mighty empire. Could the word 'climate' refer to the famous Hanging Gardens, one of the seven wonders of antiquity? The gardens were in terraces, supported by pillars, soaring to heights of more than three hundred feet above the ground – so the 'climate', in other words, was an artificial one. Either way, the quatrain bodes no good for anyone.

SUMMARY

A new cold war begins between the United States and China, thanks to brinkmanship by the Arab powers. For a time there is even the threat of a global war, but this recedes.

ISLAM DISTURBS THE BALANCE OF WORLD POWER II

2055

9 / 55

L'horrible guerre qu'en l'occident s'apreste

L'an ensuivant viendra la pestilence,

Si fort horribles que jeune, vieux, ne beste,

Sang, feu, Mercure, Mars, Jupiter en France.

❋

The horrible war being prepared in the West

Will be followed, the next year, by a plague

So terrible in its effect that it spares neither young, old, nor animal

Blood, fire, Mercury, Mars, Jupiter in France.

More rumblings of doom, specifically linked in index date to 1/55 – 2055 and 1/56 – 2056, and, by a longer tail, to 5/70 – 2070 [Global War I]. The 'plague' in line 2 is the great famine, delineated in 3/71 – 2071 [Global War V], which causes the United Kingdom to batten down its hatches and become Fortress Britain once again. In Camoëns's *Lusiad*, Bacchus, the evil demon, is the guardian power of Islam, and Mars (the personification of divine fortitude) is the guardian power of Christianity.

The link between Jupiter, Mercury and Paris is a more difficult one to run to ground, but for a long time there were two famous statues of Mercury in Paris, one by Lerambert, in the garden of Versailles, and another by Mellana in the Tuileries – and the sixth wonder of the ancient world was undoubtedly the statue of Olympian Jove (Jupiter) by Phidias, which was destroyed by 'fire' in Constantinople in 475 AD. In alchemical terms, fire is sulphur, while the three planets represent mercury, iron, and tin, respectively. France is traditionally represented by a ship.

SUMMARY

The danger of war flares up again, but is forgotten following a worldwide epidemic, which spares no one.

ISLAM DISTURBS THE BALANCE OF WORLD POWER III

Vous verrez tost et tard taire grand change,

Horreurs extremes, et vindications

Que si la lune conduicte par son ange,

Le ciel s'approche des inclinations.

✦

You will see, sooner or later, great changes occurring

Extreme horrors and vengeances

As if the moon, led by its angel

Approaches heaven and its inclinations.

PREDICTION

The angel Gabriel, in Jewish mythology, is the Angel of Death. In Islam, he is the Angel of Truth, the one who took Muhammad to heaven on Al-borak (the lightning), and revealed to him the prophetic lore. The 'moon', in this case, refers specifically to the crescent moon, symbol of Islam, which Muhammad, according to the Koran, cleaved in two to prove his mission to Habib the Wise. Referring back to 1/54 – 2054 [US/Chinese Standoff], we now find the Islamic world splitting the balance of world power in two, with China on the one side, and the US on the other, just as Muhammad split the moon – the implication being that the Islamic world will turn one nation state against the other for its own ends.

SUMMARY

A very dangerous game of brinkmanship is going on, with the West on one side, and China on the other, with the Islamic world providing the unstable fulcrum.

CRISIS IN THE ROMAN CATHOLIC CHURCH I

Que peste et glaive n'a sceu definer

Mort dans le puis sommet du ciel frappé

L'abbé mourra quand verra ruiner

Ceux du naufrage l'esceuil voulant grapper.

✣

What plague and the sword could not finish

Dies at the wellhead, struck from the sky

The abbot will die when he sees the ruin

Of those lost overboard, trying, in vain, to reclimb the ladders.

L'abbé, in line 3, is the key to this quatrain, and refers to the pope, who will metaphorically die (lose power) thanks to the schisms in his Church. The first line harks back to the past history of the Church, and to the plagues and wars it has survived over the centuries. The second line, however, shows that the crisis, this time, will come from within – from the very Articles Of Faith that underpin the Church's teachings; its 'wellhead', in other words. Once the Church loses direction, and the sense of those Articles is lost, the pope is powerless to staunch the effect this loss of faith is having on his congregation.

Line 4 is a powerful one, and portrays the Catholic Church as a ship without a crew, and possibly without a captain. The 'ladder' image is a reference to Jacob's ladder, which the patriarch saw in a vision (Genesis 28, xii), rising from the earth to heaven, and on which angels were perpetually ascending and descending.

SUMMARY

The pope dies, and the Catholic Church is thrown into disarray, with schisms and sects abounding. The Church seems to have lost its way.

CRISIS IN THE ROMAN CATHOLIC CHURCH II

Par le trespas du tres vieillart pontif,

Sera esleu Romain de bon aage

Qu'il sera dict que la siege debisse,

Et long tiendra et de picquant ouvrage.

✣

On the death of the very old pope

A Roman, in the prime of life, will succeed him

It will be said that he weakens the pontificate

That he will last long, and cause acute damage.

A direct follow-on, both in index date and meaning, from 2/56 – 2056. The old pope is dead. An Italian pope, born in Rome itself, and much younger than his predecessor, is elected in his stead. His gainsayers despair because of the possible length of his tenure as pope, and of the damage such a perceived moderniser might wreak on dogmatic tradition. They have no need to worry, however. He will be dead within a year [see 2/57 – 2057: Crisis In The Roman Catholic Church V].

SUMMARY

A much younger pope is elected, but many have misgivings as to his abilities. There is considerable resistance to his papacy.

CRISIS IN THE ROMAN CATHOLIC CHURCH III

Apres victoire de babieuse langue

L'esprit tempte en tranquil et repos

Victeur sanguin par conflict faict harangue,

Roustir la langue et la chair et les os.

✹

After the victory of the prattling tongues

The spirit quietens in tranquillity and repose

The victor, flushed with triumph, makes speeches

Roasted be his tongue, his flesh and his bones.

A direct continuation of 2/56 & 5/56 – 2056 [Crisis In The Roman Catholic Church I & II]. The wrong man, it seems, has won. He has made his way to the vacated papacy, thanks to slander and gossip. Even at the very moment of his triumph, he cannot resist lecturing his enemies. Nostradamus wishes him consigned to hell, where the devil (presumably) will give him a warm, and possibly even infernal, welcome.

SUMMARY

The new young pope tries to cement his power base too early, and alienates more people than he pleases. The cardinals are beginning to think that they may have made a grave error in electing him.

CRISIS IN THE ROMAN CATHOLIC CHURCH IV

Le soublevé ne cognoistra son sceptre

Les enfants jeunes des plus grands honnira

Oncques ne fut un plus ord cruel estre

Pour leurs espouses mort noir bannira.

✸

The raised one will not recognize his own sceptre

The children of the great ones are disgraced

Never was there a fouler, crueller being

The black one will banish their dead spouses.

Nostradamus is having another go at the upstart pope [see 4/56 – 2056: Crisis In The Roman Catholic Church III]. Almost comically, he sees the new pope as having been raised from such a low position to such a high one that he is unable even to recognize the implications and responsibilities of his own rule (*sceptre*). The faithful are disgraced, and even nuns, married to Jesus Christ, find their position in the Church undermined.

SUMMARY

Thanks to premature efforts at modernisation and reform, the new pope has alienated the middle ground. The climate is not right for such extreme measures.

CRISIS IN THE ROMAN CATHOLIC CHURCH V

2057

2/57

Avant conflict le grand mur tombera
Le grand à mort, mort, trop subite et plainte
Nay imparfaict: la plus part nagera
Aupres du fleuve de sang la terre tainte.

✤

Before the battle can be joined, the great wall falls

The mighty one is dead, dead, before his time, complaining

Born imperfect: most will now swim

Near the river the ground is the colour of blood.

The new pope dies, only a year after his enthronement. The rift in the Catholic Church is healed. Nostradamus, who consigned this upstart pope to hell in 4/56 – 2056, must be pleased. Now those who could not 'reclimb the ladders' in 2/56 – 2056, are able to swim again. The reference to 'ground the colour of blood' refers to a meeting of the College of Cardinals in the Vatican City (situated on the west bank of the river Tiber), to elect a new Holy Father, and one, this time, who unites, rather than schismatizes. The image is a striking one, and it is almost possible to imagine Nostradamus soaring above the russet convocation on a crane, *à la* Orson Welles, movie camera in hand.

SUMMARY

Extraordinarily, perhaps even sinisterly, the new pope dies. His death, however, provides the last chance to save the reputation and the following of a Catholic Church in crisis.

BUDDHISM & THE PROTESTANT CHURCH

Deux assiegez en ardente ferveur,

De soif estaincts pour deux plaines tasses

Le fort lime, et un vieillart resveur,

Au Genevois de Nira monstra trasse.

❋

Two will be besieged with burning fervour

Two full cups will not quench their thirst

The strong are finished, and an old dreamer

Will show the Genevans the way to Nira.

Nira, in line 4, could be either an anagram for Iran, or, taken as *n'ira*, it could mean 'not to go'. It could also be an abbreviation of the Buddhist word 'nirvana', meaning annihilation. *Nir*, in Sanskrit, means 'out', and the Gautama taught that the only way out from the accumulated pain we inherit each time we are reborn, is through nirvana.

Nostradamus also mentions the word 'two' on two separate occasions in the quatrain, and we know, from past experience, that this will have significance in the final reading. 'Two' was held to be the evil principle by Pythagoras, and, in consequence, the second day of the second month of the year was considered sacred to Pluto, and was unlucky, for Pluto symbolised the grave, and was the god of the dead regions. The *Genevans*, in Nostradamian code, almost invariably means the Protestants, and stems from the Geneva Doctrines of 1541, in which Calvin put forward his five great points of Calvinism.

Let's sum up the quatrain, then, given all this information: on the second day of February 2059, there will be a crisis in the Protestant Church. An elderly spiritual guide will point adherents of the old Church towards Buddhist teachings, equating the fourth point of Calvinist doctrine, namely 'particular redemption', to the fourth sublime verity of the Gautama.

S U M M A R Y

The Protestant Church has lost its direction and sense of spirituality in an ever more material world. Lessons need to be learned from the wise. A teacher will appear.

ENGLAND SECEDES
FROM EUROPEAN UNION

2060

8/60

Premier en Gaule, premier en Romanie
Par mer et terre aux Anglois et Paris
Merveilleux faitz par celle grand mesnie
Violent terax perdra le Norlaris.

❋

First in France, and now in Romania

By sea and land to the English and Paris

Marvellous deeds by that great alliance

The violent attack will lose the northern larch.

The quatrain opens with a characteristically to-the-point picture of the European Union ('the great alliance'), showing its early beginnings in France, then moving, towards England, and, later in its history (1st January 2007), even as far as Romania. Much thought has been given, during the past few centuries of Nostradamus scholarship, to the possible meanings of the word *Norlaris*, which appears in the last line of the quatrain. Most commentators agree that it must be a cryptogram for Lorraine. The answer is, in fact, much simpler than that, and relies on a simple split of the word into *Nor* (north) and *Larix* (larch). Tarver's indispensable 1849 *French Phraseological Dictionary* gives *larix* as the Latinate alternative to the French word, *mélèze*, a larch tree. Nostradamus is therefore implying that the northern part of the European tree (the United Kingdom) is lost, following a violent attack from the outside.

The word *terrasser* or *terax* means to throw a man onto the floor, or 'cut him down'. This reading is further strengthened by Nostradamus's wordplay on the conjunction of the words *Nor* and *Laris* – for the Lares were minor Roman deities, associated not only with the guardianship of the hearth and of the crossroads, but also (and here Nostradamus excels himself) of the State, in the form of the *Lares Praestites*.

SUMMARY

England has finally lost its patience with the European Union, and formally secedes. Scotland, Wales, and Northern Ireland remain as members.

SERBO-CROATIAN CONFLICT

Conflict barbare, en la cornere noire,

Sang espandu trembler la Dalmatie,

Grand Ismael mettra son promontoire

Rangs trembler secours Lusitanie.

❖

A Barbary conflict in the black gutter

Blood will be spilt, rocking Dalmatia

Great Ishmael will create inroads

In the trembling ranks of the Portuguese rescuers.

Ishmael was the eldest son of the patriarch Abraham, by his Egyptian handmaiden, Hagar. When Abraham's formerly barren wife Sarah produced a son, Isaac, she contrived that Abraham send Hagar and Ishmael away, where he became the progenitor of twelve tribes of desert nomads, and the eventual patriarch of the Shiite Muslims. The mention of Barbary, in line 1, also ties in with Ishmael, as the Barbary Coast covered much of the area (modern-day Algeria, Tunisia and Libya) in which the nomadic tribes of Ishmael dwelt.

Ancient Dalmatia lies almost entirely within what we now know of as Croatia, scene of the bloody conflict between Serb and Croat that lasted from 1991 to 1995, and that had both a racial and a religious basis, the Serbs being principally Eastern Orthodox, and the Croats Roman Catholic – both communities have significant Muslim minorities, however. The 'black gutter' in line 1 may be taken to point, therefore, to problems arising between the two races, triggered by the Muslim minority. The 'Portuguese rescuers' are most probably United Nations troops, sent in, yet again, as peacekeepers, and this takes on added significance when one bears in mind the previous quatrain 8/60 – 2060 [England Secedes From European Union], as the area concerned became part of the European Union in the first decade of the twenty-first century.

SUMMARY

A new Serbo/Croatian conflict will occur, necessitating the intervention of United Nations peacekeepers.

FRENCH LEADERSHIP

Le vieux mocqué et privé de sa place,

Par l'estrangier qui le subornera

Mains de son filz mangées devant sa face,

Le frere à Chartres, Orl. Rouan trahyra.

❂

The old man is mocked and unseated

By the same foreigner who bribed him

He will see the hands of his son eaten in front of him

He will betray his brother at Chartres, at Orleans, and at Rouen.

In ancient Egypt 'hands' were a symbol of fortitude, and in Rome they were a sign of fidelity. For a Roman to lay claim to a slave, he had to formally place his hands upon him in front of the *praetor* (chief law officer). Hands were a symbol of power over others, therefore, and for a father to see the hands of his son 'eaten' in front of him, was tantamount to seeing that son made powerless.

Chartres, Orleans, and Rouen are all cathedral cities in France, intimately connected with the laying on of power, in the form of the laying on of a crown to a future king – the implication being that, once the son has power stripped away from him thanks to his father's corruption, his brother, too, suffers at the old man's hands. In this context, both 'son' and 'brother' need not be taken literally, but may be used to imply a favoured follower, or someone being groomed for leadership.

SUMMARY

The president of France is betrayed by someone he thought was a trusted adviser. Even his anointed heir is tarnished by the scandal, and loses his position in the government.

ARAB WAR

2061

3 / 61

La grand band et secte crucigere

Se dressera en Mesopotamie

Du proche fleuve compagnie legiere

Que telle loi tiendra pour ennemie.

❖

The great army of the people of the cross

Will draw up in Mesopotamia

A smaller company, from a nearby river

Will find their rule inimical.

The earliest communities of what the Greeks knew as Mesopotamia (the land between the rivers Tigris and Euphrates) date back to 7000 BC. Geographically, the area covers the eastern part of Syria, south-eastern Turkey, and most of modern-day Iraq. The 'people of the cross', in line 1, must be taken to apply to Christians, even though we now know that the cross was also a pre-Christian emblem – Nostradamus would have been unlikely to acknowledge this fact, however.

SUMMARY

A Western army invades Arab territory. They are not made welcome.

WORLDWIDE EPIDEMIC

Mabus puis tost alors mourra, viendra,
De gens et bestes une horrible defaite
Puis tout à coup la vengeance on verra,
Cent. main, soif, faim, quand courra la comete.

✦

Mabus, though dead, returns

Both man and beast suffer terribly

Then, all of a sudden, vengeance arrives

Much blood, thirst, hunger, when the
comet passes.

Mabus is one of the cryptograms most beloved of Nostradamus's commentators. It has been transliterated into just about everything, ranging, in ascending order of lunacy, from Saddam Hussein (via Da Vinci-esque mirror writing), to 'self-abuse', the Magus, Megabyzus, Aenobarbus, Thurbo Majus, Abu Nidal, Abu Abbas, and even as far as poor old Raymond Mabus, former Governor of Mississippi and US Ambassador to Saudi Arabia (1994–96), who found himself, through mere hazard of a name, in imminent danger of being tarred as either the third Antichrist, or, worse still, one of his victims, thanks to the efforts of a decidedly mixed bag of Nostradamian conspiracy nuts. To be fair, though, no one commentator claims to have the definitive answer, and many of these suggestions are put forward with tongue solidly in cheek.

In point of fact, Nostradamus's coining of the name Mabus probably stems from something as commonplace as his knowledge of his close contemporary, the Flemish painter Jan Gossaert (1470–1532), who was known as Mabuse after his birthplace of Maubeuge, in France (situated close to Mons, and to the borders of modern-day Belgium). There may be a connection, too, with the legend of Queen Mab, the fairies' midwife of dreams, the title of queen referring, not to a regal background, but to the simple fact that she was a woman (equating with the still current Scots word *queynie*, and the no longer current Saxon word *quēn*). So could Mabus simply mean the 'time of dreams'? If that is the case, then the quatrain takes on a haunting, doomed quality, part nightmare and part hallucination. Whatever meaning we construe from it, 2062 sounds like a particularly bad time to be alive.

Summary

An epidemic that was thought to be defeated flares up again, killing many more people than before.

WARNING OF FUTURE WAR

Les fléaux passés diminue le monde,
Long temps la paix terres inhabitées
Seur marchera par ciel, serre, mer et onde:
Puis de nouveau les guerres suscitées.

❇

With the plague over, the earth shrinks

Peace will reign for a good while

People will travel through the sky, like birds,
and by sea and wave

Before war once again is called for.

Following the terrible epidemic described in 2/62 – 2062 [Worldwide Epidemic], which has decimated the world population, things will return to normal for a while. There will be peace. Travel will recommence. The word *serre* in line 3 is of particular interest here, because in Old French it means the 'talon of a bird', giving an image of people travelling through the air as if carried by a hawk – one trusts it's not invidious to remind readers, at this point, that there was no such concept as 'air travel' in Nostradamus's time. Here, he is simply taking it for granted, as if his visions had vouchsafed him a sight of the future which he accepted completely, as if it were an everyday matter.

The war in line 4, of course, is the global war due in 2070 [see 5/70], and which he warns us about, yet again, in 10/69 – 2069. It is interesting to note that in both this quatrain, and in 10/69, Nostradamus uses the word *seur*, meaning *sueur*, 'by the sweat of one's brow'. The juxtaposition of that word with *serre*, the talon of a bird, is undoubtedly intentional, and implies human, rather than God-like, will, in our mastering of the elements.

S U M M A R Y

The earth's population has drastically shrunk, thanks to the worldwide epidemic of 2062. There is a period of calm and harmony in the world, possibly as a result of collective shock.

CONSEQUENCES OF ENGLAND'S SECESSION FROM EU

DATE

2064

QUATRAIN

8/64

Dedans les isles les enfans transportez,

Les deux de sept seront en desespoir,

Ceux du terrouer en seront supportez

Nom pelle prins des ligues fui l'espoir.

❋

Children will be moved around the islands

Two out of every seven will be in despair

The land will feed those who live by it

Only the spade will unify and give hope.

Over-populated England, deprived of EU support [see 8/60 – 2060: England Secedes From European Union], will be faced with a food crisis. Children will be removed from the towns and sent into what remains of the countryside. Nearly thirty percent of the population will face starvation. Thanks to successive government policies of building houses over what remains of the green belt, not much of the English countryside survives – but those who live there, and, more importantly, those who live from it, will still thrive.

And now a short extra note on the word *pelle*, in line 4, which may provide a little insight into the method behind Nostradamus's apparent madness. To a literate Frenchman reading this quatrain in the sixteenth or seventeenth centuries, the word would have a number of connotations. The obvious one would be 'a spade'. In addition there would be the concept of the 'clerk of the pells', an officer of the exchequer whose duty was to make entries on the pells, or parchment rolls. Finally, the classically trained reader would not fail to grasp a possible reference to the 'Pellean Conqueror', Alexander the Great, who was born at Pella, in Macedonia, and which would reinforce, in line 4, the need for a strong leader to save the country from crisis.

SUMMARY

England protected in part by its geographical location from the full effects of the 2062 epidemic, finds itself faced with a food crisis. A return to the countryside is ordered, but people have become so urbanised that they no longer know how to till and harvest the land.

TREATY OF ROME

O vaste Romone ta ruine s'approche,

Non de tes murs de ton sang et substance;

L'aspre par lettres fera si horrible coche,

Fer poinctu mis à tous jusques au manche.

❈

O great Roman one, your ruin approaches

Not by your walls, but by your blood and substance

The asper, through letters, will cause such a terrible rift

Pointed steel will damage everything as far as the English Channel.

Following England's secession from the European Union [8/60 – 2060], and the EU crisis foretold in 8/64 – 2064, Nostradamus concentrates, once again, on the Treaty of Rome [see also 6/68 – 2068: Nuclear Market In Europe]. Here he shows how the main part of the 1957 treaty, that deals with the formation of the European Community, is undermined by trivial arguments about money – the asper or *aspre*, was a tiny Turkish coin worth only about the 120th part of piaster [see also 2/90 – 2090: Hungary In Crisis]. The 1957 Treaty was, of course, the 'blood and substance' of the 1958 founding of the European Community, and the 'pointed steel' mentioned in line 4 was the pen used to sign it, and also to sign the eventual documents which undermine it. The damage will be restricted to the French side of the English Channel (*la Manche*), because of England's unilateral secession from the Common Market five years previously.

SUMMARY

There is a crisis in the European Union. The original Treaty of Rome is under threat. England, no longer a member of the Union, stands apart from the row.

DANGERS OF EMBRYO REPLACEMENT

2065

9/65

Dedans le coing de Luna viendra rendre,
Ou sera prins et mis en terre étrange.
Les fruits immeurs seront à grand esclandre,
Grand vitupère à l'un grande louange.

❂

Inside the quince he will offer himself to Luna

Where he will be taken and placed in a strange land

The unripe fruits will cause great unpleasantness

Great blame, but to one, great praise.

This is a fascinating quatrain, which no commentator has come anywhere near to translating correctly. It is so full of puns and double meanings, that a literal translation would appear nonsensical. One can't help wondering if Edward Lear had not read the quatrain before he wrote 'The Owl And The Pussy-Cat':

> *They dined on mince, and slices of quince,*
> *Which they ate with a runcible spoon;*
> *And hand in hand, on the edge of the sand,*
> *They danced by the light of the moon,*
> *The moon,*
> *The moon,*
> *They danced by the light of the moon.*

Luna, otherwise known as Selene, was, strictly speaking, the full moon (the moon personified), who is in love with Endymion (the setting sun). Endymion was condemned to endless sleep and everlasting youth, and Luna comes to him, every night, upon the Latmian Hills. Their meetings are fruitful, and result in fifty daughters, but Luna is fickle, and has another few daughters with Zeus, one of whom, Erse, is the dew.

Pliny mentions that the fruit of the quince was considered to ward off the evil eye, and it is represented in many Greek statues, and also on the walls of Pompeii. Nostradamus, it has to be said, was famous for his sweet tooth, and had something of a fetish for quinces, for he was the inventor of a much lauded quince jelly, which found favour in a number of great houses due to its restorative qualities – like the fig, of course, the quince is also a symbol of fertility, or fecundity, which gives the quatrain a distinctly sexual connotation. With all this in mind, and after considerable mental debate, this particular commentator will plump for a warning, by Nostradamus, about the ethical dangers of *in vitro* fertilization.

Summary

A symbolic quatrain warning of the dangers of unfettered scientific tinkering, particularly in the form of fertility treatments. These have become so sophisticated, and so convenient, that they are threatening to replace nature – to our eventual cost as human beings.

THE EUROPEAN UNION

Paix, union sera et changement
Estatz, offices bas hault, et hault bien bas
Dresser voyage le fruict premier torment
Guerre cesser, civil proces debatz.

✳

There will be peace, union, and change

In government, high offices will fall,
and vice versa

The oldest child is tormented by preparations
for a voyage

The dispute ceases, amidst legal wrangling.

This is probably a continuation of the European Union quatrains 8/60 – 2060, and 8/64 – 2064, especially when one bears in mind the bureaucratic tangle of line 4. Triggered by England's secession from the Union in 2060, there is a massive retrenchment, in which offices go through a period of fundamental change. The 'oldest child' is no doubt a reference to France, which was the driving force behind the establishment of the former European Community, and its first signatory, alongside Belgium, West Germany, Italy, Luxembourg and the Netherlands, in 1958.

SUMMARY

The 2065 crisis in the European Union has been papered over, to everyone's relief. Now the bureaucrats are back in charge.

ENGLAND & SCOTLAND FALL OUT OVER EU

D A T E

2 0 6 6

Q U A T R A I N

1 0 / 6 6

Le chef de Londres par regne l'Americh,

L'isle de l'Escosse tempiera par gellee

Roi Reb auront un si faux antechrist

Que les mettra trestous dans la meslee.

✸

London's prime minister, ruled by America

Will freeze out the Scottish enclave

The Rob Roys will pick themselves so false an Antichrist

That they will all be thrown into the mix.

This conflict stems from England's secession from the EU [8/60 – 2060], and the schism this creates with Scotland, which resolves to remain inside the community. England will align itself with its old ally, the United States, while Scotland will align itself with its 'auld ally', France.

Rob Roy, of course, was the nickname of Robert McGregor, an amiable rogue and a splendid swordsman, who assumed his mother's name of Campbell when his clan was outlawed by the Scottish Parliament of 1662 – it didn't take him very long to become Scotland's equivalent of England's Robin Hood, though, and he only evaded transportation to Barbados by a whisker. This time the Scottish 'Rob Roys' will find that the ally they have picked for themselves is full of perfidy, and leaking with ulterior motives. Is it any coincidence that the index number of this quatrain, 10/66 – 2066, also coincides with the thousand-year anniversary of the Norman Conquest?

SUMMARY

Scotland and England disagree profoundly over Scotland's membership of the European Union. England sides with the United States over matters of trade, while Scotland sides with France.

GREAT FAMINE

2067

1 / 67

La grande famine que je sens approcher,

Souvent tourner, puis estre universelle

Si grand et long qu'un viendra arracher,

Du bois racine et l'enfant de mamelle.

❇

The great famine which I sense is approaching

Will start intermittently, but gradually become
universal

So great and so long will it be, that roots
will be torn

From the trees, and infants from their
mother's breast.

Nostradamus rarely put himself forward in the first person singular, and one is forced to assume that his purpose for so doing in this quatrain is because the content distressed him in a private and personal way. During the sixteenth century, much of France was tormented by plague, famine and warfare, and Nostradamus had first-hand knowledge of this in the town in which he had chosen to make his home, and base his medical practice, Agen. When the Black Death took not only his beloved first wife, but also his two children, the townspeople turned on him, arguing that a man who could not protect his own family from the plague was hardly likely to be able to protect others. Nostradamus packed up his bags and left, but only after he had been sued for the return of his wife's dowry by her distraught family. Impecunious and heartbroken, he dedicated the rest of his medical life to eradicating the plague, becoming one of Europe's foremost authorities on the subject. So when Nostradamus conjures up an image of starving people scrabbling in desperation at the roots of trees because the harvest hasn't been gathered in, or of infants being plucked from their dead mother's breast, he knows exactly what he is talking about.

SUMMARY

Worldwide famine follows hard on the heels of the 2062 epidemic. Its beginning is hardly noticeable, but it soon increases exponentially.

NUCLEAR MARKET IN NEW EUROPE

DATE

2068

QUATRAIN

6/68

Lors que soldats fureur seditieuse,

Contre leur chef feront de nuict fer luire,

Ennemy d'Albe soit par main furieuse,

Lors vexer Rome, et principaux seduire.

❁

When soldiers mutter mutinously

Unsheathing steel at night against their chief

Albion's enemy will struggle furiously

To upset Rome, and seduce it from its principles.

Four years after England's exit from the EU [see 8/64 – 2064], Albion's old enemy, France, seeks to foment further discord by undermining certain aspects of the two Treaties of Rome, which, in 1957, laid the basis for what was to become the European Community. One part of the treaty was called EURATOM (European Atomic Energy Community), and dealt with the peaceful uses of atomic energy, creating a single European market for nuclear materials. The key to the quatrain, and to its nuclear element, comes in line 2, *de nuict fer luire*, which, as well as meaning to 'unsheathe one's sword at night', also means, when translated literally, both 'iron that shines at night', and 'the capacity to read at night', with the inevitable implication of energy creation. One can assume from the quatrain that 'England's enemy' is seeking to force Britain out of Europe's nuclear market once and for all.

SUMMARY

Problems flare up between England and France over nuclear matters. The root cause remains England's secession for the European Union.

WARNINGS OF
GLOBAL WAR

Le fait luisant de neuf vieux eslué

Seront si grand par midi aquilon,

De sa seur propre grande alles levé.

Guyant meurdri au buisson d'ambellon.

✺

The shining deed of the newly elected elder

Will be blown south by the great northern wind

Great halls are raised by his own sweat

Fleeing, he is killed at the bushes of Ambellon.

A precursor to the global war scenario laid out in 5/70, 9/70, 2/70, 8/70 and 3/71? The index date is right, and other clues lead us towards such a supposition, most notably the symbol of the northern wind blowing south. Most commentators have always taken *seur* in line 3 to mean *soeur*, or 'sister', but it is much more likely, if taken as an ideogram, to mean *sueur*, 'sweat'.

Guyant is most probably a misprint of the word *fuyant*, 'to flee', but 'the bushes of Ambellon' remain a mystery. There is a clue, however. Bellona, wife of Mars, was the Roman goddess of war, and temples ('great halls') were traditionally built to her when war was in the offing. In classical literature, too, Bellona soon began to be linked to the moon-goddess of Asia, some time following the Mithridatic wars. The beaten Mithridates, of course, not wishing to fall into the hands of his enemies, found that he had so fortified himself with antidotes against poisoning by others, that he was unable to poison himself, and was finally forced to get a slave to stab him.

SUMMARY

There are rumblings of war, despite the placatory efforts of a newly elected leader.

GLOBAL WAR I

2070

5/70

Des region subjectes à la Balance

Feront troubler les monts par grand guerre

Captifz tout sexe deu et tout Bisance

Qu'on criera à l'aube terre à terre.

✳

From the regions governed by Libra

A great war will come, enough to disturb the mountains

Both sexes will be captured, and all Byzantium

So that cries will be heard at dawn, from country to country.

If the two countries in the Libran balance of power are the US and China, as we established in two previous quatrains, 1/54 – 2054 [US/Chinese Standoff], and 1/56 – 2056 [Islam Disturbs The Balance Of World Power], then Byzantium, by which Nostradamus would appear to mean those Islamic countries once comprised within the old Ottoman Empire, will be the ember that lights the flame of global war. The war will be a nuclear one ('powerful enough to disturb mountains'), in which both men and women will fight in combat roles, particularly on the Islamic side. At the end of the war, either lamentations will be heard, or, quite possibly, the call of the muezzin (or 'announcer'), echoing from country to country of the subjected region.

SUMMARY

The war begins, triggered by the Islamic world. The United States and China finally face up to each other in a global arena.

SUBJECT

GLOBAL WAR II

DATE

2070

QUATRAIN

9/70

Harnois trenchant dans les flambeaux cachez
Dedans Lyon le jour du Sacremont
Ceux de Vienne seront trestous hachez
Par les cantons Latins Mascon ne ment.

❁

Slicing armour is hidden in the torches

Inside Lyon, on the day of the sacred mountain

Those of Vienna will be put in the mincer

By the Latin cantons; Macon does not lie.

A continuation of the global war scenario Nostradamus begins in 5/70 – 2070, and completes in 3/71 – 2071. Macon is Muhammad, the name stemming from the poeticisation of the name of Mecca, Muhammad's birthplace, in classical and medieval romance literature, which Nostradamus would certainly have been familiar with. 'Praised (quoth he) be Macon whom we serve.' (Fairfax *trans*: Tasso, xii. 10).

The 'mountain', in line 2, is Mount Safa, which did *not*, of course, come to Muhammad: 'If the mountain will not come to Muhammad, Muhammad must go to the mountain.' Goaded on by his followers to produce a similar miracle to those Moses and Jesus were said to have wrought in testimony to their divine authority, Muhammad, irritated at the lack of belief of his followers, devised a strategy to bring them to their senses. He called Mount Safa to him, and when it refused to come, he thanked Allah, 'because it would have fallen on us to our destruction.' Here, the implication seems to be that the Western powers have called to the mountain, and it has fallen on them, in the guise of nuclear weapons – 'slicing armour hidden in the torches'. If we cast our eyes back to quatrain 5/70, of course, we also see that the coming great war will be 'enough to disturb the mountains'.

The pun on *Vienna*, and *de Vienne*, in line 3 is also a neat one. The Congress of Vienna (1814 to 1815), carved up Europe between the great powers, following the downfall of Napoleon, and the liaison of *de* and *vienne* gives us the French for to 'become' – there will be changes to the established order, therefore, as a direct result of this conflict. It is, perhaps, useful to remember that the four great powers involved in the Congress of Vienna were Austria (the Hapsburg Empire), Britain, Prussia (the German Confederation), and Russia.

Summary

Thermonuclear weapons are used on the battlefield. Whole mountains are destroyed. Efforts are made at peacemaking, but they are futile.

GLOBAL WAR III

Le dard du ciel fera son estendre,
Mors en parlant: grande execution
La pierre en l'arbre la fiere gent rendue,
Bruit humain monstre purge expiation.

❋

The spear from the skies will complete its extinguishing

It will speak of death: a terrible execution

The proud nation will be returned to the stone in the tree

Rumours of a human monster bring first catharsis, then sacrifice.

These really are an extraordinary series of quatrains [10/69, 5/70, 9/70, 8/70 and 3/71], all conterminous by index date, and all with implications of nation states brought low by global thermonuclear warfare. Why have they never been linked before? The index dates are categorical, and the symbols used are unequivocal. 'The spear (or dart) from the skies will complete the extinguishing' – a wonderful description of an intercontinental missile, for *estendre* in Old French means to 'stretch', or 'spread', and *esteindre* to 'extinguish' (the s was later replaced by an acute accent). The concept of the 'stone in the tree' means, quite literally, to be returned to the Stone Age, in which axes were made from split branches, with sharpened celts looped in for heft. The 'human monster' takes us back once again to 3/35 – 2035 and the birth of the third Antichrist (the first two being Napoleon/Stalin and Hitler). The 'seductive' leader would, by 2070, be thirty-five years old, and in the full flow of his maturity.

SUMMARY

The war is nearly over. Unparalleled destruction has been rained upon the world. Entire countries are no more. The third Antichrist makes his move.

GLOBAL WAR IV

8 / 70

Il entrera vilain, mechant, infame

Tyrannisant la Mesopotamie,

Tous amis fait d'adulterine d'ame,

Terre horrible, noir de phisonomie.

❈

He will enter, ugly, bad, and infamous

He will tyrannise Mesopotamia

Friends will pretend that the adulterous one has
a soul

The land is horrible, and black of aspect.

Is this the 'human monster' mentioned in 2/70 – 2070 [Global War III], who will bring 'first catharsis, then sacrifice'? A better description of sycophantic expediency has never been penned than in line 3's 'friends will pretend that the adulterous one has a soul'. Mesopotamia, of course, is modern-day Iraq, with a little bit of Turkey and Syria thrown in for good measure. Not much seems to be left of this former cradle of human civilization however, and far from living up to the meaning of its name in Greek as being the land situated 'between two rivers', it now seems more a case of its being the land situated 'between a rock and hard place'.

SUMMARY

The third Antichrist attempts to benefit from the fallout of the global war. People want to believe him. He makes his power base in what remains of the Middle East.

GLOBAL WAR V

Ceux dans les isles de longtemps assiegez,
Prendront vigeur force contre ennemis
Ceux par dehors mors de faim profligez,
En plus grand faim que jamais seront mis.

❄

The islanders will face a long siege

They will defend themselves vigorously

Those outside will be assailed by hunger

It will be a far worse famine than those which
preceded it.

A direct follow-on from 5/70, 9/70, 2/70 and 8/70 – 2070 [Global War], in which the US and China go head to head in a thermonuclear contest. Nostradamus often referred to the British as 'the islanders', and given the contents of 8/64 – 2064 [Consequences Of England's Secession From EU], and the implications of a British famine that is only halted by a mass return to the countryside, one could extrapolate from this that the United Kingdom remains apart from the global conflict, reverting to the Fortress Britain role that it played during World War Two. While war rages on the continent, therefore, Britain becomes self-fuelling, and self-feeding – trusting to the 'spade' [see my note in 8/64]. Those outside its borders face a terrible famine, but the United Kingdom, in a bid to save itself and its people, does not let them in.

SUMMARY

Britain has, for once, held itself aloof from the conflict. It now reaps the benefit. While a significant part of the rest of the world goes hungry, Britain has become self-sufficient, and manages to feed its own people.

GLOBAL WAR AFTERMATH/END OF PHOENIX PERIOD

DATE

2075

QUATRAIN

2/75

La voix ouie de l'insolite oiseau,
Sur le canon du respiral estage
Si hault viendra du froment le boisseau,
Que l'homme de l'homme fera Antropophage.

❖

The cry of an extraordinary bird will be heard

Canoning through the air shafts

The cost of a bushel of wheat corn will soar
so high

That man will make of man a cannibal.

Following on from the catastrophic global war of 2070 [5/70, 9/70, 2/70, 8/70 and 3/71], a terrible famine will devastate the earth, triggering the Change Of World Order depicted in 3/79 – 2079. Birds such as crows, owls, storks, ravens and swallows were considered harbingers of either good or evil (depending on breed, colour and connotation) by the augurs of ancient Greece, but Nostradamus's use of the phrase *insolite oiseau* would seem to point us towards a rarer bird – the phoenix, for instance. For Paracelsus, the phoenix symbolised alchemy, on account of the animal's ability to change its essential form through the use of fire, and for centuries the sign of the phoenix was to be found above pharmacies and chemists' shops for that reason.

Phoenix Periods (the rare occurrences when the phoenix is actually visible to human beings) range in time from two hundred and fifty years, according to Tacitus, to a maximum of one thousand five hundred years between sightings, according to the German Egyptologist Lepsius. Such sightings were deemed to herald the beginnings and ends of great human eras. If we take the length of a phoenix period to be around three hundred years, we are taken back to 1775, and the beginnings of the American War of Independence, an event that heralded both the beginnings of world revolution and the foundation of modernity. This period, Nostradamus tells us, is now at an end. Instead, we are entering an age of uncertainty and global change.

SUMMARY

The war has signalled the end of a great human era. We are entering a period of barbarism and immorality.

THIRD ANTICHRIST I

Tant attendu ne reviendra jamais

Dedans l'Europe, en Asie apparoistra

Un de la ligue issu du grand Hermes

Et sur tous rois des orientz croistra.

✺

The eagerly awaited one will never return

To Europe, but will reappear in Asia

One of the confederacy descended from great Hermes

He will grow above all other kings of the Orient.

One immediately thinks back to the series of quatrains dealing with the period 2032 - 2036 [Birth Of The Third Antichrist], when one reads this prophecy. The individual concerned, whose birth is described so effectively in 3/35 - 2035, would be forty years old at the time of this quatrain, and in the prime of life. It seems that he has survived the global war of 2070, and is intent on proving Nostradamus's prediction in 3/35, that 'the noise of his reputation will grow in the Eastern Kingdom', correct - this suggestion is further echoed in line 4 of the present quatrain, in 'he will rise above all other kings of the East'.

As if that weren't enough, we are reminded of his European origins [see 2/32 - 2032], and are now told that he repudiates them totally, and turns his face permanently towards the East. The 'confederacy descended from great Hermes' is of particular interest here, as it could imply an Hermetic link with Thoth (the Egyptian Hermes Trismegistus, scribe of the gods, and chief councillor to Osiris). Either that, or a reference back to alchemy, for Hermes was the Greek Mercury, and Milton, in *Paradise Lost*, iii, 603, calls quicksilver 'volatile Hermes'. In purely classical terms, Hermes was the god of thieves, as well as being a messenger and a herald to the Olympians, and he was also the conductor of souls to Hades [see 6/27 - 2027: Six Lucky Gamblers]. On the whole, though, it seems most likely that Nostradamus was taking the Neo-Platonist route, as the name Trismegistus means 'thrice great', and we are dealing here with the man who may well be the third Antichrist.

SUMMARY

This is the time the third Antichrist has been waiting for. From the Middle East, he moves towards Asia, widening his power base. Nature abhors a vacuum, and the Antichrist intends to be the one to fill it.

THIRD ANTICHRIST II

2077

8/77

L'antechrist trois bien tost anniehilez,

Vingt et sept ans sang durera sa guerre.

Les heretiques mortz, captifs, exilez.

Sang corps humain eau rougi gresler terre.

❂

The third Antichrist will soon be annihilated

His war will have lasted for twenty-seven years

The heretics are either dead, captive, or exiled

Human blood reddens the water that covers the earth in hail.

Could the war Nostradamus is describing really have started in 2050, when the third Antichrist was a mere fifteen years old? [see 3/35 – 2035: Birth Of The Third Antichrist]. Well, yes, it could, if the war is accepted as being one of ideological, rather than of military confrontation. There is no question here of the war having actually come to an end, but the presage in line 1 may link this quatrain to 3/79 – 2079 [Change Of World Order], in which the example of the men of Phocis is summoned up to show that all is not yet lost. The final line is one of the greatest, and yet most difficult to translate, in all of Nostradamus's writings, and conjures up, in its few, almost shunted-together words, a human and nature-driven hell the like of which we haven't experienced since the last great Quaternary Ice Age of 1.6 million years ago. The original source of the image of 'blood reddened' hail comes in Revelations 8, vii, and describes the first of the Seven Angels of God: 'The first angel sounded, and there followed hail and fire mingled with blood...'

SUMMARY

There are still some people willing to fight back against tyranny. Nostradamus describes the battle and suggests that, in the end, the third Antichrist will be beaten.

FORTRESS BRITAIN FOLLOWING GLOBAL WAR

Par arcs feux poix et par feux repoussés,

Cris hurlements sur la minuit ouis

Dedans sont mis par les remparts cassez

Par cunicules les traditeurs fuis.

✦

By arcs of fire, pitch, and flame are they repulsed

Screams, cries and shouts at midnight

They are launched from inside the smashed defences

The traitors escape through their secret passages.

PREDICTION

One is tempted to see this as a continuation of the prediction from 3/71 – 2071 [Global War V], in which the UK becomes Fortress Britain once again. There is certainly the sense of a siege here, which would make sense if Britain had become self-sufficient in food, and others wished to benefit from its bounty. It seems that the British drive off the invaders, at a terrible cost, and fifth columnists and traitors escape by the very underground passages through which they sought to undermine their own people.

SUMMARY

Britain defends its borders, and its right to isolation, against outsiders. Fifth columnists inside the island fail in their treason.

CIVIL DISOBEDIENCE BEGINS

Subite joie en subite tristesse

Sera à Romme aux graces embrassees

Deuil, cris, pleurs, larm. sang excellent liesse

Contraires bandes surprinses et troussees.

✸

Sudden joy inside sudden sadness

Will occur at Rome, of the jealously guarded favours

Mourning, cries, tears, weeping, blood, excellent joy

Opposing groups surprised and locked up.

This is a quatrain of paradoxes. Sudden joy inside sudden sadness. Mourning, cries, tears, weeping, blood, and then the unexpected use of the Old French word *liesse*, which also means 'joy'. Opposing groups, which one takes to mean groups on both sides of the argument, are surprised and locked up. This is almost a judgment of Solomon, when one comes to think about it – the sort of response a State will give if it finds itself at an impasse, facing two opposing sides who will not, under any circumstances, compromise. What Nostradamus is describing, therefore, is the beginnings of tyranny under the guise of political expedience, which, in the light of 3/79 – 2079 [Change Of World Order], will come as no surprise whatsoever.

SUMMARY

All over the world, parameters are changing. Former democratic states are arrogating despotic powers to themselves. There are mass insurrections, which are put down pitilessly.

CHANGE OF
WORLD ORDER

2079

3/79

L'ordre fatal sempiternal par chaisne,

Viendra tourner par ordre consequent

Du port Phocen sera rompu la chaisne,

La cite prinse, l'ennemi quant et quant.

✸

The locked and fated eternal order of things

Will switch direction, thanks to a new order

The old Greek order will be broken,

Its citadel taken; the enemy will not be accepted.

Given what Nostradamus predicts in the years both leading up to, and following, this quatrain, its meaning becomes all the more pivotal. It is rare for Nostradamus to generalize to such an extent, and it can only mean that he is uncertain as to the true outcome of events. Given all that, he appears to foresee what amounts to a fundamental change in the perception of democracy ('the old Greek order'). Could its 'citadel' be Athens? Or is that too literal a reading?

The 'new order' (tyranny?) does not, at the very least, find easy acceptance. Phocensian Despair, of course, means desperation which terminates in victory, and stems from the days of Philip, King of Macedon, when the men of Phocis stood alone against the united might of all their enemies. In desperation, they built an enormous pyre, meaning to immolate themselves, and their women and children, upon it. Having nothing left to lose, they then threw themselves in one final, despairing act, upon the foe, and, extraordinarily, beat them off.

Summary

The old world order has changed, apparently for good. Democracy is a thing of the past. There are many who regret its passing. Having nothing left to lose, they ready themselves for a last ditch attempt at a restoration of universal suffrage.

CLIMATE CHANGE DUE TO GLOBAL WAR

2080

8/80

Des innocens le sang de vessue et vierge.

Tant de maulx faitz par moyen se grand Roge

Saintz simulacres tremper en ardent cierge

De frayeur crainte ne verra nul ne boge.

✺

The blood of innocents, of widows and virgins

The great Red One commits many evils

Holy images are infused with the light of votive candles

Terrified and fearful, people will no longer dare to move.

Following on from the Global War of 2070 [see 5/70, 9/70, 2/70 & 8/70 – 2070], great climactic change will come upon the world. The French, at the time Nostradamus writes, held the belief that a 'red man' commanded the elements, wrecking those he condemned to death somewhere in the seas off the coast of Brittany. Legend also has it that this same 'red man' once appeared to Napoleon in a dream, foretelling his downfall. The 'Red One', therefore, is Nostradamus's euphemism for the elements, which run amok in the aftermath of a thermonuclear war, making any form of travel impossible, and rekindling, as so often happens in times of turmoil, a return to organized religion. The restoration of a communal faith was a continual preoccupation of Nostradamus's, and he returned to the subject time and time again in his writings.

SUMMARY

Fundamental climate change, triggered by the thermonuclear war of ten years back, begins to tell. People turn back to God in their uncertainty. After the horrors of an entirely man-made war, nature is now poised to take its revenge.

TSUNAMI II

4 / 80

Pres du grand fleuve, grand fosse, terre egeste,

En quinze pars sera l'eau divisee

La cité prinse, feu, sang, cris conflict mettre

Et la plus part concerne au collisee.

✺

Near the great river a ditch will form; the land will be eaten

The water will split into fifteen channels

The city falls; fire, blood, and cries conflict

Much of it caused by the collision.

When taken with 8/80 – 2080 [Climate Change Due To Global War], and 1/82 – 2082 [European Earthquakes], the 2080s do not seem like a good period to be living in southern Europe. The implication of *collisee* in the last line gives us both a 'collision', and the geographical location of the Coliseum, in Rome. A 'great river', the Tiber, runs through Rome, and Rome is situated just seventeen miles from the Tyrrhenian Sea. The Tyrrhenian Sea contains Europe's largest underwater volcano, Mount Marsili, which rears up 9,800 feet from the ocean floor. Mount Marsili was, until recently, considered dormant, but it has now been firmly established (since 1999) that the volcano is active. When Mount Marsili eventually erupts, as it most certainly will, a considerable part of the southern coast of Italy will go with it. With this in mind, quatrain 4/80 takes on a new, and far more sinister, dimension.

SUMMARY

An underwater volcano erupts beneath the Tyrrhenian Sea, causing a tsunami, which devastates the Roman peninsula.

TSUNAMI III

L'oiseau royal sur la cité solaire,

Sept mois devant fera nocturne augure

Mur d'Orient cherra tonnerre esclaire,

Sept jours aux portes les ennemis à l'heure.

✺

The royal bird will fly over the city of the sun

Seven months earlier there will be a nocturnal augury

The Eastern wall will fall, amidst thunder and lightning

For seven unremitting days the enemy will be at the gates.

This is a direct follow-on from 4/80 – 2080 [Tsunami I], and shows just how cunningly Nostradamus linked the numbers of his quatrains and their meaning, despite their nominal appearance in entirely different *Centuries* – *Centuries* being the ten separate chapters of one hundred grouped verses (apart from *Century* seven, which only contained forty-two) that comprise the main body of Nostradamus's prophecies. In this case the link is not only through the index numbers of 80 and 81 respectively, but also in more subtle ways.

Nostradamus mentions the 'city of the sun', in line 1. This was traditionally seen as Rhodes, whose tutelar deity the sun was – its great Colossos, one of the seven wonders of the ancient world, was consecrated to Apollo, god of the sun. The final line of 4/80 reads '*et la plus part concerne au collisee.*' In that quatrain, I have taken *collisee* to mean both the Roman Coliseum, and a collision. This quatrain, with its hidden echoes of 4/80, takes the environmental disasters which befall southern Europe between the years 2080 to 2082, even further south. The 'royal bird' is the Ibis, sacred to Egypt, a country situated just four hundred miles due south of Rhodes – to kill one was a capital offence. The implication here is that both Rhodes and Egypt are linked in an environmental catastrophe, whose origin stems from the shattering of the 'Eastern Wall'. The fallout from the catastrophe will continue for 'seven' days, just as the augury occurred 'seven' months earlier, and just as there were 'seven' wonders of the ancient world, which included the Colossus, and 'seven' wonders of the middle ages, which included the

Coliseum. 'Seven', of course, is a holy number, and Levitical purifications, of which this tsunami may be seen as one, traditionally lasted for 'seven' days.

Summary

Another tsunami devastates the Aegean area around the island of Rhodes, causing havoc on the Turkish mainland.

NEW LEADER
APPEARS

2081

3/81

Le grand crier sans honte audacieux,

Sera esleu gouverneur de l'armee

La hardiesse de son contentieux,

Le pont rompu cité de peur pasmee.

✹

The great scolder, bold and shameless

Will be elected head of the army

The boldness of his contentions

Will cause the bridge to break and the city to
faint with fear.

This quatrain comes bang in the middle of three terrible years in which the world order changes, and in which nature, twisted and suborned by man to his own ends, finally wreaks its revenge upon the world. This period throws up a special sort of leader – a man who harangues and scolds his people until they finally elect him head of the army. It is natural for people to seek strong leadership at a time of uncertainty, and this man provides that leadership. Coming so soon after 3/79 – 2079 [Change Of World Order], this quatrain could almost be viewed as an optimistic one, despite the worrying implications in the last line. With what nature has in store for the world, firm leadership will become a necessity.

S U M M A R Y

A brash new leader, who is, nonetheless, benevolent, comes to the fore. People, searching for miracles, turn to him. He is only a man, however, and cannot turn back the clock.

EUROPEAN EARTHQUAKE

2082

1/82

Quand les colomnes de bois grande tremblée,
D'auster conduicte couverte de rubriche,
Tant vuidera dehors une grande assemblée,
Trembler Vienne et le pays d'Austriche.

❋

When even the trees shake mightily

And the south wind seems covered in blood

So many will try to escape

That Vienna and all Austria will shake with
their passing.

Nostradamus's use of the word 'shake' on two separate occasions in this quatrain gives us our clue. An earthquake, of a sufficient magnitude to make even the greatest trees tremble, will strike central Europe, with its epicentre possibly near, or inside, the Czech Republic. The western part of the Bohemian Massif is well known for its earthquake swarms, with more than 8,000 separate quakes recorded in the period between 1985 and 1986, just one hundred years before Nostradamus's predicted date for the big one. The dust from the quake will filter and transform the sun's rays until they seem 'covered in blood', and there will be a mass exodus on such a scale that even Vienna, situated a scant few kilometres from the Czech border, will 'shake with their passing'. When, in addition, we take into account quatrain 8/80 – 2080 [Climate Change Due To Global War], with its index date of 2080, the pattern begins to fall even more firmly into place.

SUMMARY

Natural disasters, triggered by the global war, continue. An earthquake strikes the Czech Republic. Its power is so great that aftershocks are felt as far away as Austria.

LOCUST PLAGUE

Friens, Antibor, villes autour de Nice,
Seront vastees fort par mer et par terre
Les saturelles terre et mer vent propice,
Prins, morts, troussez, pillés, sans loi de guerre.

✳

Fréjus, Antibes, and the towns around Nice

Will be devastated both by land and by sea

Locusts will come on propitious winds

Kidnap, death, rape, pillage, no martial law.

More natural disasters for this apocalyptic three-year period
(2080 – 2082). If anyone ever doubted that Nostradamus's
quatrains were linked across the different *Centuries* in which
they appear, then the last few predictions, all relating to
natural disasters, and all occurring within three years of his
index dates in *Centuries* 8, 4, 5, 1 and 3, should convince them
otherwise. The Mediterranean, to put it bluntly, is in for it.
Tsunamis, earthquakes, climate change – all contrive to
create a new environment, a new landscape, almost, in which
the coastal borders of Europe are perpetually at risk. In the
bare few lines of this quatrain, an entire story emerges of
dreadful storms, followed by a plague of locusts, followed
by a total collapse of law and order, in which people go, quite
literally, mad, and only the strong, or the wicked, can survive.
It comes as no surprise to find that, just three years after
these events, the French State is entering a long-term period
of crisis [10/85 – 2085].

SUMMARY

Climatic conditions trigger a plague of locusts, but on an
unprecedented scale. The French Riviera is particularly hard
hit when the locusts are borne over from North Africa on
freak winds.

US EARTHQUAKE

9 / 83

Sol vingt de Taurus si fort terre trembler

Le grand theatre rempli ruinera

L'air ciel et terre obscurcir et troubler

Lors l'infidelle Dieu et sainctz voguera.

✿

When the sun is at 20° in Taurus, a great earthquake

Will totally destroy the packed Great Theatre

Air, sky and earth will be murky and unsettled

So that even Infidels will call on God and the saints to steer them.

The years 2080 to 2084, encapsulated in an index-conjoined series of quite remarkable quatrains, seem among the bleakest that mankind will ever have to go through. Earthquakes, tsunamis, locust plagues, and radical climate change will harry the world as a result of our own actions, and there will be a mass return to organized religion [see also 8/80 – 2080: Climate Change Due To Global War].

The next Jupiter in Taurus square to Neptune in Leo will occur in 2083. The last occurred in June 1929, a few months before the great October Wall Street Crash, which ushered in a ten-year period of unmitigated disaster for all the Western economies, and, in particular, for the United States. Nostradamus speaks specifically here of a terrible earthquake which will destroy what he calls the 'Great Theatre'. Could the 'Great Theatre' be Wall Street?

SUMMARY

Parts of New York are destroyed by an earthquake. The fall of the great buildings creates such a dense pall of smoke, dust, and debris, that for a long time the rescue and emergency services find it impossible to function.

FRENCH CRISIS PRELUDE I

Le vieil tribun au point de la trehemide.
Sera pressee captif ne deslivrer,
Le veuil non veuil ne mal parlant timide
Par legitime à ses amis livrer.

❉

The old demagogue, salt measure teetering

Will be urged never to release the captive

The old man, though not weak, does not wish
to be maligned

By legitimate means he delivers him to
his friends.

Quatrain number 10/98 – 2098 [French Crisis I] deals with the symbolical significance of 'salt', both as a concept of the vigour of the State, when the salt is kept neatly sealed up, and as an evil omen, when it is spilled or wasted. This quatrain predates that one by exactly thirteen years (thirteen is an unlucky number – traditionally, in the city of Paris, no house bears it: it was also the number present at the Last Supper, in which Judas upset the salt shaker), and points to what may have caused the French Crisis in the first place.

Trémie, in Old French, is a mill-hopper, or salt measure, and also carries with it the implication of shaking, which is generally seen as an adjunct to old age. *Vieil*, *veuil* and *veule* mean, respectively, 'old', 'wishes' and 'weak', all, once again, leading us towards the image of an elderly leader, without vigour, unsure of his ground, and minding overmuch what is said about him. The identity of the mysterious 'captive' is a moot point, but it is perhaps apposite to point out that the third Antichrist spoken of in 3/35 – 2035, would be just fifty years old at the time of this quatrain.

SUMMARY

A crisis has been brewing in France. Now it comes to a head. The aged leader hesitates, uncertain how to respond. This is a fatal mistake.

THE FUTURE OF ISRAEL

Le vieux plain barbe soubs le statut severe,

A Lyon faict dessus l'Aigle Celtique

Le petit grand trop autre persevere,

Bruit d'arme au ciel: mer rouge Ligustique.

❂

The old man conceals stern laws beneath
his beard

The Lion is raised above the wedge-shaped Eagle

The great man, small in size, persists too long

There is the sound of weapons from the sky:
the Red Sea turns Ligurian.

An extraordinary quatrain, persistently mistranslated. Suffice it to say that the 'Lion' is the emblem of the tribe of Judah (i.e. Israel). 'Judah is a lion's whelp: .... he couched as a lion, and as an old lion; who shall rouse him up?' (Genesis xlix, 9.). The 'Eagle', on the other hand, was the ensign of the ancient kings of Babylon and Persia, of the Ptolemies and Seleucides. Another link to the world of Islam is the mention of the Red Sea, which is the geographical centre of the Islamic World, running, as it does, near to the holy centres of Medina and Mecca. This is so categorical, that it comes as some surprise to find that no commentator has yet made the connection.

Perhaps it is the mention of Liguria which has traditionally lured commentators towards Italy, and away from the Middle East? But the great E Cobham Brewer tells us that the Ligurian Arts were traditionally those of deception and trickery, and this is the meaning which Nostradamus and his contemporaries would have derived from the last line. Given all this, the quatrain now begins to make sense. A literal translation would read as follows: 'The leader of Israel is a hard taskmaster/ His people have the ascendancy over the Arabs/ But he does not know when to stop.' The Arabs resort to trickery: a terrible war ensues.'

SUMMARY

Israel has still not resolved the Arab problem. Both sides find it impossible to forget or forgive the past. A forceful Israeli leader takes the initiative, triggering a fresh war.

CYPRUS PARTITION

2089

3/89

En ce temps là sera frustree Cypres,

De son secours de ceux de mer Egee

Vieux trucidez, mais par mesles et lyphres

Seduict leur Roy, Royne plus outragee.

❋

At this time Cyprus will be frustrated

In its desire for aid from the Greeks

The old will be snuffed out, both by cannon and
by distress

Their king will be seduced, their queen even
more affronted.

The Turkish invasion of Cyprus in 1974 led to the occupation of over a third of Cypriot territory by the Turks, who had ruled the island in its totality from 1571 to 1878. If one also bears in mind that the Greeks, the Ptolemies, the Romans, the Byzantines, the Franks, the Arabs, the Venetians, and the British had all ruled the island at some time or other in its four-thousand-year history, it seems that Cyprus has always been something of an Aegean powder keg.

It's no surprise, therefore, that trouble springs up again in the latter part of the twenty-first century. King Constantine II of Greece was deposed by a military junta in 1973, and Greek republican status was ratified by the electorate after civilian rule was restored in 1974 coinciding almost exactly with their partial loss of sovereignty over Cyprus. Greek history is full of surprises and upsets, and it would not stretch logic to foresee a return to a monarchy at some point during the twenty-first century. Ex-King Constantine himself has never given up his claim to the throne, and his heir, Crown Prince Paul, was born in 1967, while Paul's eldest son, Constantino, was born in 1999 – so the succession is assured.

S U M M A R Y

Cyprus still occupies the minds of the Greeks and of the Turks. The Greeks, their monarchy and self-confidence restored, attempt to reverse the partition.

US & CHINA SEE EYE TO EYE

2089

2/89

Un jour seront demis les deux grands maistres,
Leur grand pouvoir se verra augmenter
La terre neufue sera en ses hauts estres,
Au sanguinaire le nombre racompté.

✻

One day the two great leaders will become friends

Their great power will become greater

The new world will be at its highest point

The number shall be told to the red one.

It's quite encouraging to learn that after the global war of 2070, and the environmental horrors of the 2080s, human nature, in the form of personal friendship, can still make a difference. The two great leaders, of course, will be those of China and the US, and the influence of the New World (North America) will have peaked. The Great Red One has already appeared in 8/80 – 2080 [Climate Change Due To Global War], and the telling to him of the number 'two', does not bode well. We already know about the evil inferences the number two can have numerologically, from 4/59 – 2059 [Buddhism & The Protestant Church], and the linking of this number with the 'red man' who commands the elements is far from auspicious. However, it would be churlish to dilute the glory of one of Nostradamus's few partially optimistic quatrains, due only to the sting in the tail of the last line.

SUMMARY

Their confidence shaken by the long-term fallout from the global war of 2070, the new leaders of the United States and China offer each other the hand of friendship. Peace reigns for a while.

HUNGARY IN CRISIS

2090

2/90

Par vie et mort changé regne d'Ongrie

La loi sera plus aspre que service

Leur grand cité d'hurlements plaincts et crie

Castor et Pollux ennemis dans la lice.

❈

Life and death change the rule of Hungary

Law becomes more asper than duty

Their great city rings with cries and laments

Castor and Pollux confront each other
in the lists.

The *aspre* (asper) was an ancient Turkish coin, equal to about the 120th part of a *piastre* (piaster). 'Castor and Pollux', the twin sons of Leda, and brothers to Helen and Clytemnestra, were known as comazants, to sailors, when they appeared, in the guise of St Elmo's Fire, at the mastheads of ships. If only one flame appeared, the Romans called it Helen, and believed that it portended that the worst of the storm was still to come, but if two flames appeared, they were Castor and Pollux, and it meant that the storm was over.

The reference to 'lists' (tourneys) in line 4 (*lice* can also mean 'bitch', in Old French, but we can discount this), is a reference to the horses of Castor and Pollux, Cyllaros and Harpagus, which they mounted on their return from the infernal regions, and on which Nostradamus pictures them as doing battle – the implication being that if only one of them survives, the worst of the crisis is yet to come, but that if both come out of the battle equally, the crisis will be over.

SUMMARY

Hungary faces a short and sharp crisis. An unlikely concatenation of disparate forces resolves it, to everyone's surprise.

GREEK NUCLEAR ACCIDENT

DATE

2090

QUATRAIN

5/90

Dans les cyclades, en perinthe et larisse

Dedans Sparte tout le Pelloponesse

Si grand famine, peste par faux connisse

Neuf mois tiendra et tout le chevronesse.

❇

In the Cyclades, and in Perinthus and Larissa

In Sparta, and all through the Peloponnese

A terrible famine, a plague of false dust

Nine months it will last, patterning everything.

Nine is one of the great mystical numbers (along with five and three), and corresponds to the *diapason*, the *diapente*, and the *diatron* of the ancient Greeks – the trinity of trinities, in other words. This stems from the concept of man as a full chord of eight notes, and the Deity, at least according to Pythagoras, taking the ninth place on the scale, i.e. perfection. This concept of 'nine' carries through nearly all cultures, and corresponds, needless to say, with the human females' normal span before parturition. Both the Etruscans and the Sabines had nine major gods apiece, and the medieval earth was supposed to rest at the centre of nine spheres, above which came the Primum Mobile, or Heaven of Heavens.

All this to say that Nostradamus, when he speaks of a 'plague of false dust', is most probably talking of an Act Of God, rather than any man-made catastrophe. A nuclear accident springs to mind, or a worse-than-normal Melteme wind, triggered by global warming. [See also 2/3 – 2103: Global Warming/Mediterranean Famine].

SUMMARY

At some time during the preceding years, the Greeks have acquired a number of nuclear reactors. There is a meltdown of one reactor, causing a Chernobyl-like tragedy. The fallout from the disaster lingers for nine months, afflicting both the living and the as yet unborn.

TWENTY YEARS SINCE END OF GLOBAL WAR

DATE

2091

QUATRAIN

I / 9 I

Les dieux feront aux humains apparance,
Ce qu'ils seront auteurs de grand conflict
Avant ciel veu serein espee et lance,
Que vers main gauche sera plus grand afflit.

✦

It will seem to human beings that the gods

Must have been the authors of the great war

Once, long ago, the sky was clear of weapons

Whereas now, on the left hand, there is damage
still to come.

It is now twenty years since the end of the 2070 – 2071 Global War [5/70, 9/70, 2/70, 8/70 & 3/71], and the long-term fallout, both emotional, ecological. and thermonuclear, is still being felt. The war was so terrible that its seems to many observers as if non-human forces must have been involved in its inception. People look back nostalgically to a serene time when the skies were clear of hardware and tactical weapons, and, presumably, full of birds.

Nostradamus would have had no concept of the existence of either a left or a right wing in terms of politics, but he would have known, from his reading of Plato, Plutarch and Aristotle, that the left was the side of evil omens and of sinister actions, and that any signs seen over the left shoulder were considered particularly bad auspices by the Greek and Roman augurs, who reputedly studied the flight of birds for signs of future trends.

SUMMARY

Twenty years after the end of the global war, the great powers come together at a conference to consider its implications for the future of the planet. People regret the passing of the old days, and fear that further conflict is imminent.

RHONE FLOODS

8/91

Frymy les champs des Rodans entrée
Ou les croisez seront presque unis,
Les deux brassieres en Pisces rencontrees
Et un grand nombre par deluge punis.

❈

Frozen are the fields where the Rhone
enters them

Where those of the cross are nearly united

Both jackets will meet in Pisces

A great number will be punished in the flood.

A relatively straightforward quatrain predicting worse floods than usual in the Rhone estuary. The floods will be winter floods, triggered by a great freeze. The place where 'those of the cross are nearly united' is Avignon, ancient papal and anti-papal city (1309–1376), situated on the left bank of the river Rhone, and a place sorely harried by the Saracens during the crusades. The 'jackets' mentioned in line 3 are the ancient walls of Avignon, and they meet at the church of St Pierre (St Peter – the fisherman, and patron saint of fishers and fishmongers), and thus the reference to Pisces.

S U M M A R Y

Terrible floods devastate the Rhone area, following a great winter freeze.

FRENCH CRISIS PRELUDE II

2095

4/95

La regne à deux laissé bien peu tiendront

Trois ans sept mois passés feront la guerre

Les deux vestales contre eux rebelleront

Victor puis nay en Armorique terre.

✻

Their joint rule won't last long

In three years and seven months time they will
go to war

The two virgins will rebel against them

The victor is later born on American soil.

This is a categorical precursor to the French Crisis that occurs in 2098, even down to the very precise date of 'three years and seven months' ahead. The two virgins in line 3 are Joan of Arc, the spirit of French national pride [see 10/98 – 2098: French Crisis I], and Marianne, the girl with the Phrygian cap seen on French monuments, stamps, and coins, and the symbol of both Republican France and the freedom from oppression (the Phrygian cap was worn by freed slaves in Roman times).

The last line is a baffler, though. Why should the victor be born only later, on American soil? *Armorique* can also mean Brittany, but that doesn't get us much further. Unless we take America to mean 'the land of the free', and take the 'victor' to be symbolically given birth to by one, or both, of the virgins? That would mean that the true spirit of France will be recreated in the Americas, and one is then thrown back onto French separatist Canada, and the possibilities of an independent Francophile state surrounding Quebec.

SUMMARY

Trouble is still brewing in France, despite the election of a coalition government. There are fears for the future of French culture, although the Francophone outpost in Canada affords some hope.

ECOLOGICAL BURN-OUT

Les lieux peuplez seront inhabitables
Pour champs avoir grand division
Regnes livrez à prudents incapables
Lors les grands freres mort et dissention.

❈

Formerly inhabited lands will become unfit for human life

Cultivatable fields will be divided up

Power will be given to overcautious fools

From that moment on, death and discord for the great brothers.

The great brothers are *Liberté, Égalité* and *Fraternité* (Freedom, Equality and Brotherhood), symbols of the revolutionary French Republic, and known historically as the Declaration of the Rights of Man and of the Citizen. This would tend to link the quatrain to the French Crisis of 2098 – 2101, except that the verse would seem to point towards an ecological, rather than an overtly political, crisis. It's possible, of course, that the land reform mentioned in line 2 forms part of the fuse that eventually triggers the constitutional upheaval, but the global nature of line 1 might incline us to veer away from a purely parochial reading. Line 3 is a stunner, and could be applied to almost all governments and their incumbents, and is surely worthy of use as a one-off epigraph in its own right.

SUMMARY

The ecological fallout from the global war of 2070 continues, with swathes of the world left virtually uninhabitable. The quality of leadership, though, in the aftermath of the crisis, leaves something to be desired.

SECULARIZATION OF A SUPERSTATE

Celui qu'aura la charge de destruire

Templus et sectes, changez par fantaisie

Plus aux rochiers qu'aux vivans viendra nuire,

Par langue ornee d'oreilles resasie.

❋

The man whose duty it is to destroy

Fantasy-driven temples and sects

Will confine himself to the inanimate

And to those whose ears are filled with vainglory.

Who could this be? The pope? Or someone whom a nominally secular superstate commissions to eradicate dissent? Either way, it seems we are dealing with a fundamentally decent person who destroys stones rather than human beings. It's a worrying quatrain, though, and one cannot help wondering whether, rather as in Russia under Stalin, the State in question is not trying to eradicate religion in its entirety.

SUMMARY

An effort is made to eradicate religion by one of the great world powers. On a par with Stalin's secularization of Russia during the 1930s and 1940s, this tyrant, however, seems content to destroy buildings rather than people

THE MIDDLE EAST

2097

3/97

Nouvelle loi terre neufve occuper,

Vers la Syrie, Judee et Palestine

Le grand empire barbare corruer,

Avant que Phoebus son siecle determine.

❋

New laws will rule new lands

Towards Syria, Judea and Palestine

The great barbarian empire will decay

Before Phoebus concludes his dominance
of the century.

PREDICTION

Phoebus is the sun. In Greek mythology Apollo was called
Phoebos, the sun god, after the act of 'shining'. He was
regarded as the font of moral excellence, and his influence
was a benevolent one. The implication here is that moral
and ethical laws are overturned, in the Middle East, and one
is forced to refer back to 2/85 – 2085 [The Future Of Israel]
for an explanation. The 'great barbarian empire' is possibly
that of Israel, therefore, when one takes into account the
meaning of the word 'barbarian' in its biblical sense (and we
are talking of the Bible lands here). 'Therefore if I know not
the meaning of the voice. I shall be unto him that speaketh
a barbarian, and he that speaketh shall be a barbarian unto
me.' [I Corinthians, xiv, 11.]

Yet another reading could have the Arab world as the
barbarian empire, with both sides refusing to hear each
other's voice. A third reading gives us the word barbarian in
its literal, and Latinate sense, as the 'bearded one'. German
legend has it that Charles V, with his crown and sceptre, and
with all his knights and vassals surrounding him, still lives
inside the Wunderberg, on the great moor near Salzburg,
haunt of the Wild-women. His grey beard has twice encircled
the royal table, and when it grows long enough to encircle it
three times, the Antichrist will appear.

SUMMARY

The Middle East remains tinder dry, and cracks are
appearing in the entrenched positions of both parties.

FRENCH CRISIS I

2098

10/98

La splendeur claire à pucelle joyeuse
Ne luyra plus, long temps sera sans sel,
Avec marchans, ruffiens, loups oudieuse,
Tous pesle mesle montre universel.

❂

The redolent ashes of the joyful virgin

Will darken; for a long time there will be no salt

Black marketeers, ruffians, and odious wolves

Pell-mell everywhere.

Jeanne La Pucelle (Joan of Arc), was, at least according to French legend, burnt by the English, at Rouen, for sorcery, in 1431. Nostradamus's use of the Old French word *claire*, meaning ashes or bones traditionally used in refining, pinpoints the exact identity of the virgin he is alluding to, and, in addition, allows for an amusing pun on her importance as an icon of the French State – from clarity to darkness, in other words.

The entire quatrain is filled with such paradoxes, as we also have the use of the word 'salt' in line 2, which can mean either food, or, more likely in this context, 'vigour', as in Shakespeare's *Othello*, iii, 3, when Iago refers to it as '…hot as monkeys, salt as wolves in pride.' In Leonardo Da Vinci's great portrait *The Last Supper*, Judas Iscariot is known by the salt cellar knocked over by his arm, an occurrence that is almost universally acknowledged as a bad omen. Thus, when the salt of a country (France) is spilled, and its spirit (Joan of Arc) is lost, free rein is offered to every form and sort of charlatan and trickster to use the place as his playground. In this context the word 'playground' is used advisedly, since pell-mell is an ancient Italian game, stemming from *palla*/ball and *maglia*/bat, as well as its later, more common meaning, of to sink into reckless confusion.

SUMMARY

The French State, fragile for some time now, erupts into major crisis. Chaos ensues, and France loses itself in anarchy.

FRENCH CRISIS II

2099

6/99

L'ennemi docte se tournera confus,
Grand camp malade, et de faict par embusches,
Monts Pyrenees et Poenus lui seront faicts refus
Proche du fleuve decouvrant antiques cruches.

✳

The learned enemy will turn about in confusion

The mighty army sickens, brought low by ambush

Both the hills of the Pyrenees and of the Apennines will be closed to him

Old containers will be discovered near the river.

A follow on, perhaps, to 10/98 – 2098 [French Crisis I]? There is an echo of biological warfare here, as the 'mighty army sickens', and sinister sounding 'old containers' are found near a river – however this may just as well be meant metaphorically, the 'mighty army' implying past glories, and the 'sickening' being one of the soul. It is also possible that the 'learned enemy' in line 1, is linked to the 'enemy' in 10/1 – 2101 [French Crisis IV], who doesn't keep his part of the treaty. In this case, all four quatrains must be taken together to form a worrying whole for the French State.

SUMMARY

The French crisis intensifies, and the army is called in. The intervention is ineffective, and the crisis worsens.

FRENCH CRISIS III

Longtemps au ciel sera veu gris oiseau,

Aupres de Dole et de Touscane terre

Tenant au bec un verdoyant rameau,

Mourra tost grand et finera la guerre.

✦

For a long time a grey bird will be seen

High above Dôle and Tuscany

Holding in its beak a flowering branch

The great one will soon die, and the war
shall end.

The grey bird is an arrow, winged with grey goose feathers: 'The grey goose wing was the death of him,' goes the ancient proverb. A dove, representing the human soul, traditionally flew from the mouths of saints at their death. The death foretold is probably that which occurs in 10/1 – 2101 [French Crisis IV]. An alternative reading would have the grey bird as the dove of peace, holding an olive branch in its mouth – the dove, in conventional Christian iconography, signifies the Holy Ghost.

SUMMARY

One of the leaders who triggered the French crisis is about to die. His death will bring peace.

FRANCO-BRITISH CRISIS

Dedans les isles si horrible tumulte

Bien on n'orra qu'une bellique brigue

Tant grand sera des predateurs l'insulte

Qu'on se viendra ranger à la grand ligne.

✺

A horrible tumult in the islands

Soon only the warlike cabal will be heard

So great will be the predators' insults

That a great league will form against them.

PREDICTION

Given the French Crisis described in 10/98, 6/99, 1/100 & 10/1
– 2098–2101, and given France's proximity to the United
Kingdom, and given the fact that Nostradamus habitually
referred to the British Isles as 'the islands', it doesn't exactly
beggar the imagination to suppose that the 'predator', in
this case, might be France. If, in addition, we take into
account the very specific mention of Joan of Arc, in 10/98,
and the long-term grudge held by the French against the
British for her alleged burning at Rouen (other French
sources have her as marrying the Sieur des Armoise, at Metz,
with whom she went on to have a family), then the
likelihood becomes even greater. Nostradamus is not, of
course, implying that France is going to invade Britain, or
any such nonsense, but merely that there will be a severe
falling out between the two ancient rivals. When one
remembers that England acrimoniously seceded from the
European Union in 2060 [see 8/60], then this quatrain makes
all the more sense.

SUMMARY

France, irritated by its own problems, turns its attentions
to external matters, in an effort to placate its people. A rift
is contrived between France and the United Kingdom.

FRENCH CRISIS IV

A l'ennemy l'ennemy foi promise
Ne se tiendre les captifs retenus
Prins preme mort et le rest en chemise,
Damné le reste pour estre soustenus.

✳

A treaty between enemies

Isn't kept: the captives aren't released

The leader is captured and killed, his remains
are stripped

The rest are damned for sustaining him.

Prediction

We're a very long way from home here, and apart from translating the quatrain as accurately as possible, it is very
difficult to tease out a precise prediction. The quatrain is so
close in time to the last three, that they are almost certainly
connected.

Summary

Despite its efforts at diluting its domestic problems by
means of a contrived spat with the United Kingdom, France
is finally forced to face up to the root cause of the recent
crisis. One of the main protagonists is dead – the other is
brought down too, despite his last-ditch attempts at trickery.

GLOBAL WARMING IV/ MEDITERRANEAN FAMINE

Pour la chaleur solaire sus la mer

De Negrepont les poissons demi cuits

Les habitans les viendront entamer

Quand Rhod, et Gennes leur faudra le biscuit.

✦

Due to the sun overheating the sea

The fish from Negroponte will be par-boiled

The local inhabitants will claim them

While people in Rhodes and Genoa are starving.

Negroponte was the Venetian name for Evvoia (Euboea), a Greek island in the Aegean Sea famed for its sulphur springs. Like Rhodes and Genoa, it changed hands numerous times during the course of history, and it is perhaps this which provides the connection Nostradamus is seeking – mention, however, must also be made of the village of 'Gennes' in France, on the Loire river, a few kilometres to the north of Saumur, but it would probably be tendentious in the extreme to try to engineer some extreme connection between there, the Ligurian Sea, and the Aegean.

If we accept the first reading of Genoa, then, it seems that Nostradamus is describing a catastrophical increase in global warming, to the extent that a relatively shallow sea like the Aegean (at least where it shelves towards the land), actually begins to boil its own fish. The word *entamer*, too, is an interesting one, because, as well as encroaching on a person's rights, it can also mean to make a cut or a graze in the flesh, both symbolically and in real life. Putting all these disparate elements together, *à la* Sherlock Holmes, we are left with a dreadful scene of starvation and privation, which the islanders of Evvoia refuse to alleviate.

SUMMARY

After a disastrously hot summer in the Aegean area, crops are spoiled, and there is widespread famine. The shallower parts of the Mediterranean become like pea soup, and fish, with nowhere to escape to, are parboiled in the heat.

SUBMARINE WARFARE

Quand dans poisson fer et lettre enfermée

Hors sortira qui pis fera la guerre

Aura par mer sa classe bien ramée,

Apparoissant près de Latin terre.

❋

When a letter is enclosed inside an iron fish

The man who emerges is entitled to make war

His fleet will travel beneath the boughs
of the sea

Reappearing near a Latin land.

The key word in this quatrain is *ramée*, which, in Old French, means 'beneath the boughs' or 'under the trees', with the emphasis being on something which 'shelters'. When this is conjoined with 'the sea', and an 'iron fish', what Nostradamus is talking about becomes pretty obvious – a fleet of submarines. The Latin land is probably Latin America, although it could equally well apply to Spain or Italy.

SUMMARY

A diplomatic crisis is triggered at the United Nations. A fleet of submarines is sent to quell the disturbance, with permission to make war if the situation warrants it.

NOSTRADAMUS
TAKES HIS LEAVE

Vingt ans du regne de la lune passez,
Sept mil ans autre tiendra sa monarchie,
Quand le soleil prendra ses jours laissez,
Lors accomplit a fine ma Prophecie.

❂

Twenty years after the moon's reign is over

Another monarch will take over for seven
thousand years

When the sun finally takes its leave

My prophesying will be accomplished.

The moon (*móna*) in Anglo-Saxon means a 'measurer' of time. In Sanskrit, Gothic, Old French, and Greek, the moon was viewed in a similar way, and in the true tradition of right-brain (insight, imagination, musicality, art awareness, 3-D forms, left-hand control) and left-brain (reasoning, science, language, number skills, right-hand control) functionality, it was considered a masculine and left-brained, rather than a feminine and right-brained force, by, amongst others, the Arabians, the Slavs, the Hindus, the Mexicans and the Lithuanians.

The sun, on the other hand, and particularly in Celtic and low-Breton mythology, took on a feminine aspect, and lived in perpetual fear of being eaten by the wolf, Fenris (hence eclipses). The Celts believed that the sun would one day have a daughter, who would reign in her stead, rekindling the life force of a weary world. John Donne has this to say about the duality of the sun and moon:

> *Here lyes a shee Sunne, and a hee Moone here,*
> *She gives the best light to his Spheare,*
> *Or each is both, and all, and so*
> *They unto one another nothing owe...'*

[An Epithalamion On The Lady Elizabeth And Count Palatine, vii, 1–4].

Nostradamus is now telling us that we have come to the end of that particular era of Manichean Dualism, and that we must prepare ourselves for Armageddon, and a subsumation into Haeckelean Monism, or the Universal All. The End, in other words.

Summary

The human period in world affairs is coming to an end. It has lasted for a very short time, and will leave no imprint whatsoever of its passing. Nature will fill the vacuum left by humanity.

ARMAGEDDON/
THE FINAL PROPHECY

DATE

7074

QUATRAIN

10/74

Au revolu du grand nombre septiesme,

Apparoistra au temps jeux d'Hecatombe,

Non esloigné de grand d'age milliesme,

Que les entrez sortiront de leur tombe.

❂

When the great number seven completes itself

Games will begin at the Tomb side

Not far from the turn of the Millennium

The dead will rise out of their graves.

Seven is the holy number, and equates, symbolically, with a span of length – the beginning and the end of things. Just as there are seven ages in the life of man, and seven bodies in alchemy, and seven spirits of God, so there have been seven great eras in the life of the earth. These are now over.

Nostradamus's use of the word *jeux* (games) in line 2 is an odd one, but then we remember the Greek concept of the playfulness of the gods [see 8/16 – 2016: Ecological disasters II], and the image is no longer so surprising. The final dating of Armageddon presents some difficulties, as we do not know if Nostradamus is dating his seven-thousand-year span from the inception of Man, or from the birth of Christ. Either way, the world is moving inexorably towards its end, and the sum total of our human achievements will be neither significant, nor remembered, in its aftermath.

SUMMARY

The joke is on us. Everything humanity thought would last will be lost in the mists of time. We are simply part of a whole, and relevant, even to ourselves, no longer.

When we to be to be begunne,

we did beginne to be undone.

ANON

INDEX

Page numbers in **bold** indicate main
 entries